Fire Someone Today

What others are saying about

Fire Someone Today

"Bob's book is like a year's worth of lunches with someone who has been way down the road and taken a lot of lumps—who can now help you avoid repeating his mistakes. And you only have to buy once."

—GUY KAWASAKI,
Author, *The Art of the Start*

"Made you think! And that's more than you can hope for from the typical business book, that's for sure. Everyone who manages anyone needs to think about the stuff inside."

—SETH GODIN,
Author, *All Marketers Are Liars*

"Bob Pritchett has written a classic for anyone running or starting up a small to midsized business. There's compelling information on every page. I couldn't stop reading, and the same will happen to you."

—PAT WILLIAMS,
Senior Vice President, Orlando Magic

"I've watched companies such as Microsoft and RealNetworks grow to be powers in the industry. I've also started two businesses myself. Bob's advice is direct, accurate, and honest. Even Bill Gates would have appreciated a copy in his early years! It's no wonder Bob has built such a successful business for himself, one which combines his personal and professional passions."

—BRUCE JACOBSEN,
Founder/CEO Kinetic Books

"*Fire Someone Today* is a breakthrough for those of us that hate wading through theoretical business books when we really want to read practical, actionable commentary. As founder of multiple businesses, I found the material fresh, accurate, and fraught with humor. A must-read for every start-up CEO."

—KEVIN CABLE,
Serial Entrepreneur and Cofounder,
Cascadia Capital

"Incredible insight into the basics of building a successful business, regardless of size."

—MARK ANDERSON,
President,
Anderson Hay & Grain Co., Inc.

"*Fire Someone Today* is a practical, revealing, and immediately useful guide for any entrepreneur or CEO of a startup or any small company, regardless of the level of success and experience of that leader. It is a guiding torch for the treacherous road of new businesses creation and development."

—Lotfi Belkhir,
Founder/CEO,
Kirtas Technologies, Inc.

"Bob's 'true confessions' is a refreshing and unvarnished look at the life of an entrepreneur. Many lessons learned and shared in this jewel of a publication."

—Paul J. Grey,
CEO, AudienceCentral

"*Fire Someone Today* is full of practical wisdom and advice. The book is entertaining, truthful, and very useful. I recommend it to every business person of any size company."

—Alan Schell,
Past President, Upchurch Scientific

"I've attended countless seminars and read numerous books over the past thirty-five years, trying to be the best I could be as an entrepreneur and employer. Sadly, most of those books and seminars were more 'academic' than practical and worth far less than the time and money I invested. *Fire Someone Today* is a refreshing exception! The practical 'nuts and bolts' approach makes this a must-read for any serious entrepreneur, especially one who is just getting started or who is even contemplating launching a new business."

—Robert E. Martin,
Founder/Co-Founder and CEO,
Heritage Management Services, Inc.,
Advantage Home Care, Inc., Advantage
Rehab, Inc., Mid-South Medical
Supply, Inc.

"I recommend *Fire Someone Today* for anyone who has a business of their own, or is considering starting one. Bob's observations, experiences, and recommendations make it a lot easier to see what we so often are missing when we are so close to our own businesses."

—Robin Halliday,
CEO, Rivetek Inc.

Fire Someone Today

And Other Surprising Tactics for Making Your Business a Success

Bob Pritchett

NELSON BUSINESS
A Division of Thomas Nelson Publishers
Since 1798

www.thomasnelson.com

Published in Nashville, Tennessee, by Thomas Nelson, Inc.

Nelson Books titles may be purchased in bulk for educational, business, fund-raising, or sales promotional use. For information, please e-mail SpecialMarkets@ThomasNelson.com.

This book does not constitute legal advice. The author is not an attorney. Every business situation is unique, and laws differ by jurisdiction. This book should not be used as a substitute for competent legal counsel specific to your location and circumstances.

Pritchett, Bob, 1971–
Fire someone today / Bob Pritchett.
p. cm.
Includes bibliographical references.
ISBN 0-7852-1262-0 (pbk.)
1. Small business—Management. 2. Executive ability. 3. Leadership. I. Title.
HD62.7.P745 2006
658.02'2—dc22 2005030055

Printed in the United States of America

06 07 08 09 10 RRD 5 4 3 2 1

To My Parents

Table of Contents

Introduction

Entrepreneurs are the underappreciated heroes of civilization. Virtually every advance in art or science has been either in the service of business or has reached us through the work of an entrepreneur.

Entrepreneurs are the people who publish and promote the artists. Entrepreneurs are the people who make the results of accidental discoveries available to everyone. Entrepreneurs are the people who seek out new and better solutions.

Writing was developed to keep business records. The seas and continents were explored in order to find new business opportunities. In pursuit of profit, entrepreneurs have given us the steam engine, the electric light, and one-hour dry cleaning.

The march of progress has been to the beat of the business drum. Entrepreneurs are the drummers.

Being an entrepreneur is the greatest job on earth.

Small Business Is Hard Work

The greatest job on earth is a very hard job. The people who are starting and running businesses are, quite literally, running the world. And that takes a lot out of you.

The world is not run by the United Nations. The world is not run by the president of the United States. The world is run by the people who run the businesses that milk the cows, build the widgets, drive the trucks, and sell the goods.

Wal-Mart, General Motors, and the rest of the Fortune 500 do a lot of the heavy lifting. But small businesses have a harder job.

Big businesses are huge machines. They are well documented, well staffed, and they know what to do and how to do it. Yes, they are complex. Yes, they can fail. But, for the most part, the people running them understand how the machines work and have the resources to keep them going.

Small businesses, and the entrepreneurs and business owners who run them, are building new business machines. These new machines are a lot harder to operate than the big established businesses. Small businesses are

- **growing faster.** Changes in revenue, number of employees, etc., are occurring at a breakneck pace in small businesses.
- **innovating more.** Large businesses may invent new products, services, and processes too, but they do not have to invent their business model and processes on the fly.
- **taking bigger risks.** Small businesses are financed with credit cards, personal guarantees, and loans from family and friends. Starting a small business is not just a risky career step; it is a risky life step.

Small businesses do not come with an instruction manual. The small business leader has no guideline for operations, no procedure to follow, no boss to consult, and no leadership training institute at the posh corporate retreat center.

Small business leaders have to find their own help. And some of the best help is the experience of others. That's what I have to offer.

Who I Am

I am an entrepreneur. I am actively leading Logos Research Systems, Inc., a business I cofounded more than a decade ago. At the time of this writing, we have around ninety employees and $9 million in sales, a subsidiary in South Africa, and hundreds of thousands of customers in more than 140 countries.

I have purchased several companies and negotiated to sell my own. I have raised money from family and friends and through a formal private placement. I have a partner and minority shareholders. I took my company through an initial public offering and then canceled and unraveled the deal before we broke escrow.

I have lived through years of 100% growth and years in which we shrank. I have had to lay off people. I have had a million dollars in the bank account, and I have been overdrawn and owing a million.

I am not a professional speaker. I do not write business books for a living. I am not an angel investor, venture capitalist, or business consultant. I am not an academic trying out new business theories. And I do not have an MBA.

I have made a *lot* of big mistakes. From them, at last, I have learned enough to see strength, stability, and success in my business. And I am not done yet: the business is still growing, and I am still making mistakes.

I will never run a billion-dollar business. The business I'm in doesn't have a big market, and I am okay with that. I will not do whatever it takes to get ahead. Though I fail sometimes, I try to put my faith, my marriage, and my family ahead of my ambition.

I am telling you all of this to establish my credentials for writing this book: I am not a celebrity CEO. I am not a one-in-a-million business genius. I am not on the outside looking in. I am the guy down the street who is working hard, running a pretty good business, and who has learned some lessons that may help you too.

The Purpose of This Book

In my travels down the entrepreneurial road, I have been blessed in many ways. I have gotten a lot of good advice. I have read a lot of good material. I have learned from the experiences of others. And, most importantly, the mistakes I have made were bad enough to teach me valuable lessons but not bad enough to kill my business. (It was a *very* fine line.)

The purpose of this book is to share some of what I have learned with you, my fellow entrepreneur, business leader, and hero of civilization.

This book is not intended to be inspirational. It is intended to be useful. It is not full of business platitudes or step-by-step how-to advice. If you want to be told that if you dream it, you can do it, get another book. If you want to know how to write a business plan, don't look here. I do not have "Thirteen Incontrovertible Laws of Excellence."

This book is about what to do, what not to do, and why. (Names and details about many of the people who appear in this book have been changed to protect the innocent. And the guilty.)

When my business was just starting up, I knew a guy who worked for a lawn care service and was participating in a multilevel marketing business. Every time I ran into him he wanted to "talk business," which to him meant parroting phrases from motivational tapes.

"There is nothing better than to wake up in the morning, look into the mirror, and say, 'Hi, boss!'" he said.

"What are you talking about, you soap-peddling, wannabe entrepreneur? You spend your day cutting lawns for someone else's business. When I look into the mirror, I ask, 'Are we going to meet payroll?'" I replied.

Okay, not really. I said, "You're right."

It *is* great to be the boss. There are some nice perks to being an entrepreneur. But it is often a hard, lonely, and frightening responsibility.

You are the one who has to come up with the new ideas. Entrepreneurs clothe and feed and entertain and supply the world, creating the wealth and the jobs. You are the one who provides the place where people can work and grow to their greatest potential.

In these pages you will find tips that can help your business grow, warnings that can keep you out of trouble, and encouragement to make the tough calls. It is my hope that through this book I can provide to you, as so many others did to me, that one piece of advice that makes all the difference. Please be sure to visit the Web site, www.firesomeonetoday.com.

You have the greatest job on earth, and I want to help you to keep it and to enjoy it more.

1 Fire Someone Today

John was not making it in sales. Not in frontline sales to customers and not in relationship-based sales to resellers. John was not a good fit for technical support or administration either.

John was a great guy, and I couldn't bear the thought of firing him, so when a position opened up managing the shipping department, we put John there.

Costs began to rise in shipping. John needed more staff than the previous manager had. Personality conflicts emerged, and soon I was regularly leading long meetings where we worked on issues—costs, quality, personalities—that the department had never had problems with before.

Having already moved John through the whole company, there was only one more move to make. John had to go.

I dreaded firing him. I worried about what he would do, where he would find work in our small town, and how he would support his family. In my mind I took on all his responsibilities as my own. I put off the event for as long as I could until it was clear that the costs and conflicts were endangering the whole organization.

What a relief it was when I finally fired John. Shipping ran smoothly, and costs were reduced. All it cost me was a small burden of guilt and failure. I thought I could carry that weight until one evening when my mother told me she had run into John's wife at the grocery store. I cringed.

"John's wife told me how glad she was that you let John go," my mother told me. "It forced him to think about what he really wanted to do, and he has decided to go back to school and prepare for ministry."

What a relief! I had not ruined John's life. And what a waste, I later realized. In my foolish desire to take responsibility for John, I had helped keep him from his true calling for as much as a year after it was clear to me that he was in the wrong place.

Who Should I Fire Today?

If you have more than a handful of employees, then you probably have some who need to go. The reasons they need to go are varied; each employee is a unique individual and special in his or her own way. Fortunately, we have some big bins you can toss them into for easy sorting.

- **Whiner.** The whiner is happy only when he is unhappy. The whiner is not engaging in constructive criticism and is not taking initiative to address problems. The whiner is just relentlessly complaining. At best the whiner simply annoys everyone around him with his silly, petty complaints. More often he sucks joy out of the organization like a massive leech of discontent.
- **Slacker.** You will find slackers all over the office: standing at the coffee machine, sitting at other employees' desks, and lounging with the newspaper in the lobby. Occasionally, you will even find slackers at their desks—surfing the Internet.
- **Incompetent.** The incompetent are often well behaved, eager to please, and disciplined in their work. They just don't do it very well.
- **Troublemaker.** The troublemaker stirs up discontent and actively works to create "us versus them" divisions throughout

the organization: between you and your employees, between individual employees, between departments within the organization, and even between the organization and the customers. More dangerous than self-absorbed whiners, troublemakers set up conflict even when they are not a party to it.

- **Misfit.** The misfits are just in the wrong place. They may have a good attitude, good work habits, and even great skills. They just don't get the indefinable *it* that is the key to success in your organization. Or worse, they do get *it*, but *it* is something they don't really care about. They think they can care if they try hard enough, but it is hopeless. Their hearts are not in it.
- **Redundant.** The innocent of the group, the redundant is the number two person in a job that one person can do well. Ideally, redundant employees can be moved into other positions, but when that is not an option, it is important to see them for what they are: a wasted resource. The waste is not just of your resources either: if their work is superfluous, then they are wasting their time in a job with no growth or prospects.

How Do I Know When to Fire?

If you already have someone in mind, today is the day.

If you are thinking you need to fire someone, then you probably already have tried to address your concerns about his or her performance in other ways. In order to be certain that firing is the right step, it is good to review the ways in which you already have tried to address the problem. Did you

- explain the position and what is required of the employee?
- provide training on equipment and procedures?
- conduct informal reviews of performance and outline areas that need improvement?

- discuss conflicts and differences with coworkers and try to resolve them?
- ask the employee what he thinks of his performance and how he believes it could be improved?
- conduct a formal performance review and record the review in writing?

These are important steps in helping employees succeed, but they have usually been exhausted by the time you start thinking of firing them. You are thinking of firing them because you already know in your heart that it is time for them to go. Follow your instinct.

Why Are We Reluctant to Fire People?

There are lots of bad reasons that we are reluctant to fire people.

- **We want to be kind.** Firing people seems mean.
- **We are concerned for the employees.** We take on too much responsibility for the employees and think that we are protecting them from financial difficulty, emotional distress, embarrassment, etc.
- **We don't want to admit that we made a mistake in hiring.** After investing so much time and money in advertising and interviewing to fill a position, it seems like a personal failure if the hire doesn't work out. Especially if we "sold" this hire to other managers or bragged about the new employee's credentials. Or worse, if we sold the position to the candidate who is now the employee we need to fire.
- **We have a large investment in training.** We would rather throw good money after bad than write off the bad.

- **We don't know how we will fill the position.** Somebody has to do this job, and if we fire this person today, who is going to do the job tomorrow? We don't have anyone else to fill the position nor the time to find them.

These are not just bad reasons; these are selfish excuses. Compassion is caring about others, but retaining the employee who should be fired is all about caring for ourselves—it is never about the employee. We want to protect our investment, our presumptuous feeling of parental responsibility, our time and energy, even our reputation for "being nice."

If employees quit, or were hit by the proverbial bus, we would find a way to address any real issues related to their sudden absence—we would have to, because their departure date would be out of our control.

The past is also out of our control; we can't go back and not make the hire, not spend on the training, or not create a "mission critical" job function. By firing we can at least make today the day we start investing in the future instead of continuing to waste resources and to delay the inevitable.

What Happens When We Don't Fire

When we don't fire employees who need to be fired, we are doing a great disservice to the employees, their coworkers, and ourselves.

We are sending the employees a message: "You're no good." Even when we don't say those words, we are communicating the message in our silence. Because when we hold back on firing someone, we aren't just holding back the negative "You're fired" message; we are holding back all the subtle positive messages that encourage and motivate people every day.

- We are not telling the employees that they are doing a good job.
- We are not giving them promotions or pay increases or bonuses.
- We are not letting them work on the most important projects or with the most important customers.
- We are not putting them in a position to be appreciated and respected by their peers.

We are sending the employees' coworkers a message: "You don't need to do a good job. We don't distinguish between good work and bad around here, so don't take the trouble to do things right, or fast, or at all. There is no penalty for really bad performance and probably no reward for really great performance. Nobody is watching."

Our employees know, often better than we do, who is and is not pulling their weight and contributing to the organization. They are looking at us to see how we address poor performance or deal with people who are misplaced in the organization.

We are poisoning our own attitudes. Our own attitudes change as we develop a feeling of pride about our "mercy" in retaining the employees while, at the same time, resentment grows for what we perceive are their responsibilities and our wasted time and resources. This chilling of the heart will reveal itself in icy blasts at the employees and their coworkers.

In truth it is our responsibility as managers and bosses to act, not the employees'. When we don't fire appropriately, we are wasting everyone's time. The employees are delayed in their pursuit of a better-suited job. The organization suffers from waiting for the right person for the job. And we damage our own authority and effectiveness by failing to perform our own job: properly managing our limited resources.

How to Go About Firing Someone Today

As important as it is to fire when necessary, you first want to make sure that it is necessary. As a last resort, you should think about retaining the employee in a different position—effectively firing the person from the current job but hiring her for another one. For an employee in the "misfit" bin, this can be a way to retain your investment in finding, hiring, and training.

Don't use a change in job description or an in-company transfer to avoid a necessary firing, but be sure to evaluate them as options. Firing someone should not be about the person, but it should be about the poor pairing of the person with the job. Don't let the necessity of firing an employee from her present job prevent you from seeing possibilities for her success in a different position.

Ron seemed like someone who would be a great salesperson. He had energy, charisma, and a passion for the product. He just wasn't doing a very good job in inbound telephone sales.

We moved Ron to outbound telephone sales to retailers, but his performance didn't improve. The only bright spot was his success at building a relationship (and sales) with a group he'd gone to visit in person.

We didn't have any other sales positions and could not afford to keep Ron in a position where he was not succeeding. Before firing him, we talked about what we could do that used his skills since telephone sales was such a poor fit. We decided to build on his in-person success and created an experimental, new position. Within a short time, Ron created a new channel—in-person presentations at conferences—where he consistently tripled the sales of the best telephone salesperson.

If you don't have a job in which the employee could succeed, the next step is to talk to your attorney.

As expensive as it is to talk to your attorney, it is a lot more expensive to make a mistake in the process of firing someone. In the minimum billable portion of an hour, you can review the circumstances of and potential problems with the planned firing. It is a great investment, at least until you are completely familiar with the issues and have a formal process in place.

Even if you have become something of an expert on employment law and are widely known as "The Axe," you will want to consult your attorney before firing anyone who might have grounds for a complaint or, just as important, who might be inclined to make a complaint, grounds or not.

Be Prepared

You need to be completely prepared before actually firing someone.

Consult your attorney or internal guidelines and make sure that you are not going to violate any employment or discrimination laws. Check any relevant employment contract for special notice or severance pay requirements.

Inform the various staff members or departments (payroll, security, network administration, etc.) who may need to know of the firing beforehand in order to cancel security codes and network access and to calculate final compensation.

The most important preparation is to be firmly decided. The meeting where you fire someone is a presentation, not a negotiation.

When you announce that you are firing someone, you are taking your professional relationship with that person over the edge of a cliff. There is no way back to the top of the cliff; there is only pathetic grasping at branches on the way down. The employee may suggest a change in job description, different working hours, or reduced compensation, or may ask for another chance to make improvements in her performance. You have reviewed all these options before deciding to fire, so you can clearly and politely explain that the decision has been made and that there is nothing to negotiate.

Your presentation should use the minimum amount of time required to address the maximum list of issues. Think of it as a concise PowerPoint presentation with little time for questions. (Actually using PowerPoint to fire someone is a bad idea.)

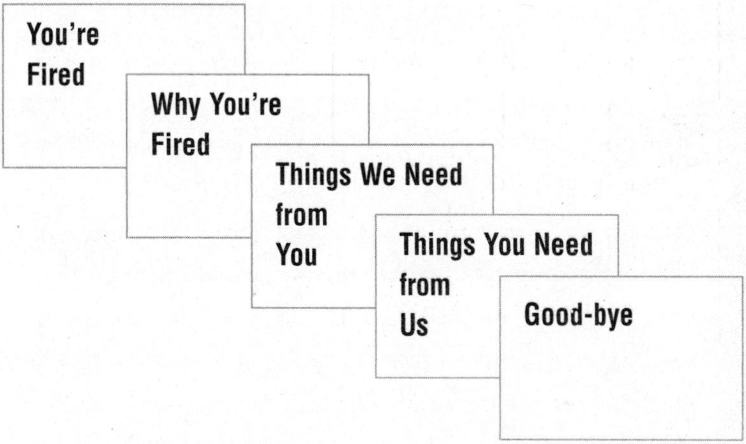

If you have followed the right steps before firing people, it won't be coming as a complete surprise to them. (Unless you are firing them because they can't see things coming.) It is imperative that you give only a short, verbal reason for firing someone. Don't elaborate, and don't put it in writing. Imagine that there is a Miranda warning for supervisors:

> You have the right to remain silent. You have the right to an attorney. If you can't afford an attorney, you are wrong because you can't afford not to have an attorney. Anything you say will be recorded, discussed, analyzed, dissected, twisted, and thrown back at you in a court of law and in the eating and drinking establishments where your employees congregate.

A checklist can help ensure that you don't forget anything and that your presentation addresses as many questions as possible. Items on the checklist should include the following.

- **The reason.** Explain why you are firing the employee. Be concise.
- **Effective date.** Explain that the firing is effective immediately. (It should *always* be effective immediately.)
- **Return of company property.** Ask for immediate return of all keys, employee ID, equipment, etc. Have a checklist prepared for items the employee may not have on his person and a deadline for their return.
- **Review of agreements.** Provide copies of confidentiality and noncompete agreements the employee has already signed.
- **Benefits status.** Provide a written explanation of the status of her benefits and the procedures involved in continuing health benefits, moving or cashing out retirement accounts, etc.
- **Final compensation.** Have a check prepared for everything owed to the employee (salary, commissions, accrued vacation time, etc.) through the end of the day.
- **Severance.** If you choose to offer a severance payment, you may have the option of providing it in exchange for a release against any complaints related to the firing. You should not require the employee to sign the release at the firing meeting; give him a day or two to review it and take it to his own attorney if he chooses, and then pay the severance on the return of the signed agreement and all company property.
- **Personal effects.** At the conclusion of the meeting, you should ask the employee to gather her personal effects and leave. You don't want to delay this or give the employee access to the facility later without supervision. If you escort people to their desks

> and then to the door, people may think you are cold. But if you let them hang around long enough to erase files, take the customer list, or send a nasty e-mail to the whole company, people will just think you are stupid. Cold is better than stupid.

Planning and preparation make a difficult process easier for everyone involved.

After the fired employee leaves, you should announce his departure to his coworkers. A simple e-mail or statement like "Today was John's last day with the company" is enough.

Firing Is Healthy, Normal, and Necessary

In *Good to Great* Jim Collins talks about how great companies focus more on "who's on the bus" than on where the bus is going. The right people will point the bus in the right direction, and they are up to whatever challenges you will encounter.

The value of having the right people on your bus is pretty obvious. The hard part is kicking off the wrong people—and it is just as important. The wrong people are sitting in seats that could be used for more of the right people. And the longer the wrong people are on your bus, the further they will eventually have to backtrack in order to get on the right bus for them.

> When we don't fire someone we should, our inaction is malicious. We are hurting our organization and wasting the employee's time on a job with no future. Our motivations are most likely selfish; at the very best, we are just being stupid.

I firmly believe that for all employees with a "fire-me" problem, there are jobs where they can excel and be happy and where they will receive the positive reinforcement that comes with a job well done. Set them free to find that job starting today.

2 You Are the Reason You Are in Business

My friend Ken is a brilliant engineer. His success inventing things like engine mounts for commercial jets helped him move into a house on Seattle's Lake Washington with a dock and a boat.

Ken's plans for a waterfront lifestyle—hopping in the boat to visit friends and waterfront restaurants—were slowed down by the hassle of using his slow and awkward boat lift. It was not long before he designed and built a zippy, new solar-powered lift that could put his boat in or out of the water in fifteen seconds at the click of a garage door opener.

After waterfront neighbors started inquiring about getting their own lifts, Ken and his wife, Deborah, took their lift to a local boat show to gauge interest. Interest was through the roof. They were deluged with orders, and Sunstream Corporation was born.

Success meant that Ken and Deborah had to build a team of salespeople, assemblers, installers, and engineers to keep up with demand. Customers clamored for lifts in various sizes and with all kinds of specialized accessories. Ken found himself with less and less time for engineering as he was drawn into promoting the company, building a sales channel, raising money, and dealing with the administrative needs of a high-growth business.

Ken hired the best people he could, and as the company grew, he gave managers responsibility for the company's various departments so that he could focus on the company as a whole. It worked well, except in the engineering department.

The engineering was competent, but Ken was frustrated by the slow pace and uninspired solutions. The staff needed days to do what he could do in hours, and their work did not reflect the elegance of his original design. Still, he told his friends, having put a manager in place and given him complete responsibility, it did not seem right to meddle with the details of specific engineering problems—especially since he was already so busy with the bigger issues of building and running the company.

Ken was nuts.

Every business needs to raise funds, promote its products, and service its customers. Every business needs to watch accounting and overhead and inventory. Every business is the same in every way except for the reason it is in business. In an entrepreneurial company, that reason is the entrepreneur.

Before Sunstream, there were plenty of competent engineers at lots of good companies building slow, clumsy boat lifts. The market did not need yet another me-too product.

Sunstream was created because Ken is a brilliant engineer. When growth caused Ken to take a hands-off policy toward his engineering department, he took away its reason to exist: his unique talent.

It Is All About You

Why did you start your business? You started it to do something your way. You wanted to offer a particular product or sell a particular service or run something a particular way. When you start a business, it is all about you: your idea, your talent, your passion. Even if the business is designed to serve other people, you are starting it to serve them the way *you* want to serve them.

When you are starting out, it is easy to make sure everything is done your way—there is no one else to do it. As you grow and bring others into the business, though, your company will change into something that reflects the many talents, strengths, and weaknesses of your team. This is the time when you need to be particularly vigilant to make sure your business remains what you want it to be even as it grows into its own identity.

Never Stop Owning the Heart of Your Business

What sets your business apart from XYZ Corporation? Why did you start your own business instead of continuing to work for someone else?

Whatever that thing is, it is the heart of your business. It is why you are in business, and it is what sets your business apart from every other. You need to consider this your personal domain and continue to oversee it personally, no matter how large your organization becomes. It is also important that you maintain your personal competence in this area.

Bill Gates set a great example in this area by taking the title "Chief Software Architect" at Microsoft. Despite being the richest man in the world and having tremendous skills in many areas of business, Gates has never stepped away from supervision of (and competence in) Microsoft's core function of software development.

Even when Microsoft had thousands of employees and Gates was a busy CEO with responsibility for the entire organization, software developers would tell of receiving middle-of-the-night e-mails from him with a comment or question on their source code.

The message was incredibly clear: software development was still at the heart of what Microsoft did, and Bill Gates was still the keeper of the heart. Everyone knew that Gates was watching the software-development process. They knew it was important to him, and they would not be able to pull the wool over his eyes on technical issues.

Owning the heart of your business ensures that your business retains its reason to exist. It ensures that your employees and customers understand what the business is about. It keeps you aware of the health of the organization and helps you command the respect you need in the marketplace in order to sell your products.

Put Your Fingerprints All over It

Your hands should be wrapped around the heart of your business. But don't forget to put your fingerprints all over the rest of the business too. If you don't care, who will?

As the founder and head of a company, every aspect of the business and its operations reflects on you. You are responsible not only for yourself but for all of your employees and their actions on behalf of the company.

This is much more than making sure they do not make promises or sign contracts you do not approve of. It is making sure you are happy with the way your offices look, the way your phone is answered, the way your receivables are collected, and the way employees decorate their e-mail signatures.

I am not suggesting you micromanage every part of your company. I am suggesting that you do not consider any part of the company off-limits to micromanagement. By regularly reviewing and tweaking details throughout the business, you keep yourself up-to-date on operations and ensure that your business reflects you.

From My Way to the Company Way

As the leader of a business, you need to have the confidence to say, "We are doing it my way," and the wisdom to know when your way needs to change. Eventually your way will need to grow into the company way.

When my partner Kiernon and I started Logos Bible Software, we were both programmers. We had a talent for design, and we could both write code very quickly. My weakness was that the code I wrote tended to not be very well tested. Together we put amazing products

Over My Dead Body

Everyone running a business should have a few nonnegotiable positions. I am not talking about issues of right and wrong like, "We do not pay bribes to win contracts." I am talking about points of personal preference like, "We will never have fewer than twenty-five chocolate chips in each of our cookies," that you designate as issues of right and wrong. Or, better yet, life and death.

Once you have chosen your nonnegotiable positions, you should make it a point to bring them up regularly and demonstrate your utter devotion to them. Rant and rave if you must. Hold fast against every appeal to reason or emotion.

Your intractability on these points serves to illustrate that no matter how much authority has been delegated in your organization, you are still ultimately in charge of even the tiniest details. And if your points are well chosen to reinforce your vision of the organization, they will help communicate that vision to your employees and customers.

- Apple Computer's Steve Jobs is infamous for his insistence on a one-button mouse (to promote his vision of simplicity) in a world where the average computer mouse has two to five buttons and a wheel.
- The mustachioed Walt Disney enforced his vision of amusement-park-friendly personal grooming by prohibiting Disney employees from wearing mustaches, a ban that lasted years after his death.
- Sam Walton, founder of Wal-Mart, believed that working in a retail business meant working Saturdays, and so he regularly held meetings on Saturdays, even for headquarters-based executives.

At my company I insist on having a person, not a machine, answer the phone. No number of sales pitches for "automated call distribution" or appeals based on call volume can sway me from my position that great customer service means answering customer calls in person. If a computer answers your call to Logos Bible Software, you will know I'm dead.

into the marketplace quickly, but we left a lot of the debugging to the first batch of customers.

We were one of those software companies whose version 2.0 would blow you away—and would blow your computer away too. Cautious users waited for version 2.1, and if you were still scared, you could always hold out for version 2.1a, b, c, etc. In one release things did not stabilize until the "g" version.

Kiernon left the company right before a planned rewrite of our entire software platform. His departure gave me the dangerous freedom to single-handedly impose my "fast and loose" programming style on the new platform.

In the years since we had started the company as two programmers in a basement, we had added a number of other very talented programmers. I appointed one of these programmers, a strong advocate of process and documentation, as the project lead. I knew that our users' patience had limits and that we needed more discipline in our programming. At the same time, I felt that left completely in the hands of the new lead, our software development would lack the cutting-edge innovation and quick-release cycles that were key to our success.

Months of conflict followed as I stubbornly stuck to "my way" of software development. Even though I knew he was correct about many of the weaknesses of my way, I would not give the project leader the freedom to implement his way. Software development was the key function of our company, and I knew that my way of doing it was what made the company what it was, for good or for bad. I was not going to turn that over to someone else.

Over time I helped the project lead to see that some of the things he felt were weaknesses in our way of doing things actually played a role in our success and differentiated us from our competitors. He helped me to see which parts of our process needed to be changed and could be changed without detracting from our strengths. Together we redefined my way as the company way.

It Is Not Our Way, It Is the Company Way

On the path from *your way* to the *company way* watch out for detours into *their way.* If you let them, your employees or, worse, your customers will take over your business and redefine it for their own purposes.

When you start a business, you *are* the business. Whether you start as a sole proprietor or a large venture capital-backed start-up, you as the founder define the business and dictate how it will be run. You can rightly say, "The business is mine." As the business grows and you add employees and customers, there is a temptation to transfer the authority to define the business to the many people who participate in it and to say, "The business is ours."

Resist that temptation. The business is yours until it can stand on its own; it should never be someone else's.

Always think of your company as a single person. Many entrepreneurs think of their companies as if they are their children. It is a good model. Your company starts as an infant, an extension of yourself for which you make all decisions and for which you act as the sole representative. As it grows to maturity, it emerges as its own person and develops its own values and ways of doing things.

You do not want your company's values dictated solely by the people it is presently associated with any more than you want your children's values dictated solely by their friends. In both cases you want to see your values serve as the basis for your offspring's—wisely informed by time and advice from employees and friends, customers and acquaintances.

As your company grows, it should develop its own personality. It should have values and ways of doing things that define it as an organization. As a company and as a brand, it should develop an identity independent of yours and of all your employees. The staff will turn over, and you may sell or leave the business. The organization may outlive any one person's involvement; it will become an independent entity.

HP, Nordstrom, Wal-Mart, and Dell are some of the many companies where the vision of the founders to do things "my way" grew into a shared vision to do things "the *company-name* way."

Strong corporate cultures usually come from founders (or succeeding leaders) who build a business their way—who have their fingerprints all over every piece—and who then manage to turn their way into their company's way.

Establishing the Company Way

In the early stages of your new leadership, you need to be able to articulate and explain your way, and you need to be clear about how important it is. Otherwise, it can turn into a productivity bottleneck. And trying to establish your way as the company way in an existing organization might prove to be even more difficult.

As you make decisions that reflect your way of doing things, you should be explaining the *why* of the decision to the people involved. If there is a rationale behind the *why,* you should explain it. "We ship every package overnight because it reinforces our speedy image." If the *why* is arbitrary, feel free to use the parental classic: "All of our stationery will be triangular in shape *because I said so.*"

Your explanations should be as repetitive as possible, to the point of being catchphrases:

"... because we are the premium product ..."
"... because fewer controls is better design ..."
"... because the customer is always right ..."
"... because we stand for quality ..."
"... because we will never be undersold ..."
"... because white shirts look clean ..."

As the company grows, you need to be open to ideas on how to improve or change your way. Maybe overnight shipping is too expensive and triangular stationery gets stuck in the mail-sorting machines. Listen and make changes where necessary, but do not give up the responsibility for defining the way.

Hand off decision making to others as soon as possible but only once you know that they have absorbed your way of making those decisions. When you hear employees using your catchphrases to explain something or to argue a point, you will know that you have established a company way.

Assert, Protect, and Grow

Ken got back into the details of his engineering department. He got rid of the antiquated design ideas that his engineers had brought in from their previous experience. Ken got involved in teaching the engineers what it was about his designs that set Sunstream's products apart from the competition. He explained the principles behind his designs and helped his staff create new work that reflected those principles.

To build Sunstream Corporation, Ken had to assert and protect his role as the brilliant engineer whose work defined and distinguished the company. To grow it he needed to turn *Ken's way* into the *Sunstream way.* That successful transition embedded Ken's way of doing things in the corporate culture. It also helped ensure that Sunstream could grow larger than Ken could ever manage alone without losing touch with its reason for being. Today the *Sunstream way* is a great success.

3 Nobody Loves Your Baby Like You Do

I have seen some ugly babies. I have seen newborns with pointy cone heads and disturbing coloration. I have seen infants who look like old Uncle Harold. Not all babies are beautiful.

What is beautiful is the way that the parents of all these babies look at them. The parents see the babies through the lens of hope, full of potential. It doesn't matter if a baby looks ready to play the alien offspring in a sci-fi flick; to mom and dad even the most hideous baby is beautiful and loved.*

Your Business Is Your Baby

Your business is your baby. You conceived it, gave birth to it, nurtured it, and protected it. You sacrificed to meet its needs, and you taught it how to live. Like any parent, you can see beyond your baby's flaws to its fantastic future. And it's frustrating how your baby's potential isn't clear to everyone else.

You may have a great business. You may have a great product. You may provide a great service. But nobody is going to love your business, product, or service as much as you do. Nobody else can see things the way you see them. Nobody loves your baby like you do.

*I was blessed to not require such self-deception. My children were beautiful from the moment they were born.

Colonel Harland Sanders's baby was Kentucky Fried Chicken. And nobody loved Kentucky Fried Chicken like the colonel did. Even though his business model consisted of franchising the chicken recipe and cooking process to other restaurant owners, the colonel considered every batch of Kentucky Fried Chicken his own. In his autobiography, Colonel Sanders tells the story of a franchisee who took it upon himself to use a different cooker than the colonel had prescribed.

Colonel Sanders, then around seventy years old, got in his car and drove to the offending restaurant, arriving early in the morning. After backing his car up to the kitchen, he went in, crawled under the counter, and removed the franchisee's cookers. He hauled out the barrel of KFC spices and left a message for the owner: "Tell him he's out of the chicken business as far as Kentucky Fried Chicken is concerned. I've pulled his cookers, his spices, everything he's got, and he won't represent me anymore."[1]

Even after selling the company, Colonel Sanders continued to travel for and represent KFC until his death in 1980 at the age of ninety. His passion for his business—his baby—was so strong that he represents it still, more than two decades later.

The Vision Thing

How you see your business is your vision for the business. You don't just see it as it is, or even as you'd like it to be. You see it off in the future—what it's going to be. Nobody can match an entrepreneur's passion and enthusiasm for her business. Nobody else has the clarity of vision for what the business is going to become.

Communicating your vision and getting others to see your business through your eyes is one of your primary responsibilities. You need to help others see your baby as you see it: grown and mature, strong and beautiful.

As the founder or CEO, it is not enough to just have the vision. You need to be the leading communicator of and cheerleader for the vision. You need to be sharing your vision inside and outside the organization. It doesn't matter if you don't have a charismatic personality or if you aren't much of a salesperson. There is no substitute for passion and sincerity, and no one else can match yours. You are the number one salesperson for your business whether you realize it or not.

Does this mean you should be out pounding the pavement and writing up orders? Not necessarily, though it doesn't hurt to keep up that skill. What it does mean is that you should never give up the role of leading spokesperson for your vision. You should never delegate the job of helping people see through your eyes. You can get help, and others can share your vision, but it will never belong to them like it does to you.

Apple Computer cofounder Steve Jobs is famous in the technology industry for what's called his "reality distortion field."[2] Jobs's charismatic personality and ability to get others to see things his way is so powerful that employees would attempt (and often accomplish!) impossible tasks at his urging. Investors, customers, and the press believe the ridiculous when he asserts it.

Steve Jobs is Apple's number one salesperson and the chief communicator of Apple's vision. In fact, Apple's vision for technology is largely Steve's vision for technology. Apple has whole departments full of marketing flacks and public relations experts, but Jobs is the person they put onstage to announce a new product or technology because no one else can communicate his vision with his passion.

I don't have Steve Jobs's charisma. I'm not a great salesperson. For years, I sent others out to talk about my company and to call on customers because I thought they could do it better than I could. And in most ways I was right.

- The people who handle press relations at my company do a great job. They're patient and persistent, and they never forget details.
- The salespeople who work for me do a great job. They listen to customers, overcome objections, and ask for the sale.

I'm not very good at any of those things, so I tried to leave them to others. Sometimes circumstances would force me into talking about the company or trying to make a sale. I wasn't very smooth in those situations, but I found that I got pretty worked up as I started talking about the company and my vision for it. To my surprise, the people I was talking to did too. My passion and excitement were doing what my technique could not: building enthusiasm in others and closing sales. I was able to get others excited about my product and business because they could feel my passion and sincerity.

> Passion sells vision. Turn on your own reality distortion field.

My Baby Looks Like Your Baby

If everyone is saving their love for their own baby, how do you get more love for *your* baby? The answer is showing people how taking care of your baby is taking care of their baby too.

There are only three groups you need to show:

- Vendors
- Employees
- Customers

For each group you need to take the time to see things from their perspective and to find out what's important to them so that you can position your vision—your baby—as an important element of their own.

Vendors. The companies that sell you products or services may be passionate about what they make or their special business models. But you are important to them primarily in terms of how much you purchase from them. So look for vendors for whom your business will be an attractive baby.

I used to think that the smart move was to buy from the biggest vendor: computers from the market leader and audits from the most prestigious accounting firm. But my business was nothing to these giants, and I often got poor service. Smaller vendors valued my business more and gave me better service.

Big Law Firm: Billed the minimum quarter-hour for every five-minute phone call. Billed a quarter-hour for the five-minute call I made to point out they'd accidentally billed 2.5 hours, instead of 0.25, for the last five-minute call.

Small Law Firm: Doesn't bill for five-minute calls.

Big Accounting Firm: Held audit hostage for 25% more than agreed-upon fee because "it took longer than we expected."

Small Accounting Firm: Delivered bill and suggested I pay the full amount only if I was satisfied with the work because they didn't want any unhappy customers.

Choosing a vendor of the right size is one way to ensure that your business is important to your vendor. While smaller vendors don't have the resources of a larger one, they are more likely to have a passion for your business and to see your success as essential to their own.

You will have the most success with vendors for whom you represent at least 5% of their business. Of course, you may never be that important to some vendors: UPS and the telephone company may never see you on their top-twenty customers list. In those cases you want to find an account rep (or even a third-party broker) for whom you can be a 5% account. That way your baby is your vendor's baby too.

My friend Bob cofounded Consumerware, a consumer electronics company. Consumerware didn't actually build products. It designed them, specified the parts, and then sent the projects to a manufacturing company for production. Then Consumerware would sell the finished products.

There are a lot of different parts and technologies in something as simple as a telephone. Very few firms have the resources to create every part of a device from design to production. A modern telephone includes plastic, computer hardware, software, displays, a microphone, speakers, etc. Different companies specialize in making the various components. The enormous size of the consumer electronics market means that there are hundreds of companies providing parts and services.

This ecosystem of supporting companies allows a small firm like Consumerware, with less than a dozen employees, to design and bring to market products that compete with those of multinational firms like Sony, Panasonic, and General Electric. It also makes it very important to choose the right partners.

Consumerware's experience with two specific partners highlights the importance of choosing partners who are more likely to love your baby the way you do.

For LCD screens, Consumerware went to one of the largest manufacturers in the industry. Their size, and the fact that they supplied the LCD screens used in some of the world's most popular electronic devices, gave Consumerware confidence that they'd chosen the right partner.

The manufacturer had all the capability that Consumerware needed and was even able to create an LCD screen specifically for Consumerware's new flagship product, a high-end cordless telephone. It would only take a month.

But at the end of the month, the LCD screen wasn't ready. And it wasn't ready at the end of the next month, or the one after that, or after that. In the end, it was six months before the screen was ready. Why? The production run for Consumerware's thousands of LCD screens was bumped to the bottom of the list by an order for millions of units from a multinational firm.

Consumerware didn't have a huge product line. The cordless telephone was its baby and the center of its plans for the year. Sales of older products were tailing off, and the delay in releasing the new cordless telephone created serious financial difficulties.

Fortunately, for final manufacturing of the telephone, Consumerware had chosen to stay with the contract manufacturer it had worked with for years. This manufacturing firm didn't have lots of huge clients: Consumerware was its largest and represented 30% of its business.

Consumerware's growing problems were of no interest to the large LCD manufacturer. Consumerware's business was like a rounding error on one of its larger invoices. If they lost Consumerware's business—or even if Consumerware went out of business—it wouldn't make much of an impact on the manufacturer.

In contrast, Consumerware was the most important account at the smaller contract manufacturer. If it lost the Consumerware account, a big hole would be left in its own business.

When Consumerware went to the contract manufacturer, explaining the situation and the problems created by the delay of the cordless telephone, it received a very sympathetic ear. The vendor quickly gave Consumerware the extension under the terms requested and even offered to make a significant loan on favorable terms so that Consumerware wouldn't have to sell equity in order to weather the cash-flow crunch the delays were creating.

Consumerware's new cordless telephone was its baby—and the contract manufacturer's baby too. Had Consumerware been unable to make it through the cash crunch and ship the telephone, the manufacturer would have lost its largest client.

Employees. As a cofounder of my company, I see the whole business as my baby. I care about everything that touches on the business, and I think about it all the time. In the early days, everyone involved was a stakeholder; we worked long hours and stayed up all night, planning, talking, and dreaming. We shared an all-consuming passion for the business.

As the company grew and added employees, I was surprised to discover that many of the new hires didn't share our obsession. In fact, they acted like working at the company was a lot like having a job rather than being on a world-changing mission.

I concluded that these people were lazy slackers.

Later, I read a magazine article by an entrepreneur which said that it is okay for your employees to go home at 5:00 p.m. because *they don't own the company.* This startling revelation prompted me to find out why some of the employees *did* work so hard and why they seemed to view the business like I did.

What I discovered was that everyone—both the slackers and the diehards, as I simplistically categorized them—had the same basic aim: advancing their own goals.

The slackers had goals that were independent of the business. They weren't really slackers; they were just using the job as a way to pay the bills so that they could do what they really wanted—community theater, in one case.

The diehards—the people I thought shared my passion for the business—were also pursuing their own goals, not mine. It just happened that what they did to pursue their goals overlapped with what was needed to pursue mine.

- One hardworking intern was focused on having a job lined up after graduation and was putting in extra hours to impress everyone. His "all-day-and-night" work habits were an investment in learning as much as possible from the internship and in ensuring he was at the top of the list for a full-time position after graduation.

- A software developer was focused on being established as the designer of the software instead of being stuck implementing someone else's design. He was putting in extra effort in order to be the first to work on each new component, ensuring that he would get to lay the design foundation for that area before anyone else got to it.
- One of our clerks was focused on increasing her salary in order to buy a house. Her new enthusiasm for taking on more responsibility was driven by the need to hit a specific salary level in order to meet the requirements her mortgage lender had set.
- Many of our employees are regular users of our primary software product. The extra effort some of them were putting into it came from a personal desire to make it better for their own use—and in some cases to implement new features from their personal wish lists after hours.
- The "all-night, every-night, always-at-the-office" types turned out to be mostly single guys with no social life. They were at the office for lack of anything more interesting to do, and while they were always available, they were often spending those extra hours on ping-pong and computer games.

Over time, many employees cross my subjective line from slacker to diehard and back again, depending on how their goals line up with mine. Sometimes the goal alignment is temporary: the intern's need to win a job offer or the clerk's need to earn a mortgage-qualifying salary. In other cases, there is a longer-term alignment: the developer's desire to own the software design or an intrinsic need to work on challenging projects or to do quality work.

Try to learn more about what motivates your employees and to show them how what the company does, and how the company prospers, can advance their own personal goals, whether they are financial or lifestyle goals. Learn to look for employees whose personal goals are compatible with the business's goals. You want to hire people who have career ambitions that can be satisfied in your growing company and who enjoy the challenges of the work you do. They should share a passion for the products or services you provide and have personal goals that working with you can help advance.

It does not matter whether your employees are passionate about money or project ownership or the personal satisfaction of quality work. It matters that you can show them how taking care of your baby is taking care of their own baby too.

Customers. The design of my company's software is beautiful. I am a technology guy at heart, and I am in love with our product. It is clever, elegant, and extremely versatile. If my customers understood how beautiful this software is from an architectural point of view, they would buy it simply as a piece of art.

Unfortunately, only a handful of software developers and I understand it. And my attempts to communicate the inner beauty of our product to others have only led to a lot of standing alone in the corner at social events.

My customers are primarily pastors. Pastors have two major responsibilities: spending time alone studying in preparation for preaching sermons and teaching classes, and spending time with other people in counseling, hospital visits, and hosting events. Pastors work long hours and are always on call. They aren't interested in the beauty of my software product. They are interested in freeing up time.

When I first started out, I tried to sell my product on what it was to me. It didn't work. To sell software to pastors, I have to focus on what's important to them, not what's important to me. It's not enough—and it's often pointless—to show them what a great product my software is. I need to show them what benefits they get from using the product.

When pastors use Logos Bible Software, they can do a better job of sermon preparation, consulting more books and resources in less time than if they had used paper books. The time they save is put back into their ministry and family life. That saved time is what is important to my customers.

Every sale is ultimately about the benefit to the customer. Many companies focus on selling the merits of their product, leaving the translation from product attributes to customer benefits for customers to figure out on their own.

Does anyone really care if the gasoline has additive XYZ-99 or if the cheese was aged ten years? Only as far as that means their engine will run cleaner and require less maintenance and that the cheese will be sharp and tasty. Don't leave it to the customer to make the translation. Your product is your baby; your customers will never love it like you do, so show them how your baby looks just like theirs.

Seeing Through Another's Eyes

When I see an ugly baby in his mother's arms, the beauty is in the mother's eyes, not the baby. Parents can tell you the significance of every little thing about their baby and spin the smallest progress into a wonderful event. And it works. I am able, in a small way, to see beauty in every baby—even the ugly ones—through the eyes of the parents.

Help others to see your baby—your business, product, or service—through your eyes. Don't be afraid to share your passion, and don't give up responsibility for seeing and communicating your vision.

Look through the eyes of your vendors, employees, and customers in order to learn how to best help them see through yours. Find out what babies they love, and show them that their baby looks a lot like yours.

4 There Can Be Only One—Plan for Your Partner's Departure

When I was a teenager, I toured a factory and met its owner. Dreaming of having my own business, I asked him for the best advice he could give me. His response was two words: "No partners."

When I started the business I run today, I did not take his advice—I started it with one partner and soon added another.

Starting a business is hard work, and having a partner made it a fun adventure rather than a lonely quest. We did everything together, from the paperwork to set up the business to sales calls to taking all of our meals together so we could work on the business every waking hour. We became best friends and worked well together for years. When the day came that my original partner decided to leave the business, though, we realized that our lack of planning had endangered the multiyear investment we had all made and had changed the nature of our personal relationships.

There is no way I could have started the business or seen it grow the way it did without my partners. As much as I now believe that "no partners" was great advice, I know that a partnership is sometimes the only way you can launch and build a business. But if that is the case, you need to make planning the end of your partnership part of planning the start of it.

Choose Your Partners Wisely

Partnering with someone to own and run a business is the biggest relationship commitment you can make outside of getting married. Entering into a partnership is committing to spend a lot of time with someone for a very long time. You may spend more waking hours with your business partner than with your spouse. When you enter into a partnership, you are risking your career, money, credit, reputation—and possibly your sanity—on your partner.

In considering a partner, you should look for someone who brings something valuable to the partnership and who is willing to share the long-term risk with you in pursuit of the same long-term reward.

- **Partners should have long-term value.** To build your business you will need money and skills. Do not partner with someone to get money or skills you could borrow or hire for a season. Partner with people who bring financial resources you could not otherwise acquire or who have a deep set of skills you will need for the long-term.
- **Partners should be willing to share the risk.** Business involves risk. Everyone in a partnership should have a similar appetite for risk, whether it is large or small.
- **Partners should have similar goals.** Why are you in business? For independence? For money? For a cause? Identify your goals and only partner with people who share them. Review your goals often to ensure they are still aligned.
- **Partners should have similar values.** What wouldn't you do for the business? What about your partner? Beyond the obvious issues of ethics and legality (you do not want a partner who would break the law or ruin your reputation to advance the business), you should look for compatibility in

what you value. Will your partner put the same value that you do on family, health, and free time? Will your partner meet your standards for sacrifice, and will you meet your partner's?

- **Partners should anticipate inequity.** Avoid frustration and recriminations. Acknowledge at the start that your partnership will be inequitable in ways that you cannot foresee and be prepared to accept it. Over time you will discover that some partners invest or sacrifice more than others and that the contribution of some partners turns out to be less important or useful than was anticipated. It is one of the many risks in business—deal with it.

What Does It Mean to Have Your Own Business?

Does your partner think it means the same thing you do? Does being your own boss mean working one hundred hours a week to build your business or the freedom to play golf all day every Wednesday? You and your partner should agree on the how as well as the why of building your business.

Friends and Family

The desire to partner with people we know and trust leads many people to enter partnerships with friends and family members. For every horror story I have heard about ended friendships or split families, I have heard a success story too.

I believe that the key to partnering with friends and family members is being clear about which relationship will take priority. When disagreements or tough decisions arise, will the business or the personal relationship come first? Are you willing to have the personal relationship end in order to advance the business? Are you willing to sacrifice your desires for the business in order to maintain the personal relationship?

Agree on the Partners' Roles

There are lots of roles to play in a business and many ways to share responsibility. You can divide things into good cop/bad cop, inside/outside, production/sales, creative/numbers, pictures/words, or any number of other categories.

Whatever roles you choose, be consistent. Employees, vendors, and customers all need to know with whom they are dealing and that decisions by one partner in his area of responsibility will not be contradicted by another partner.

If you are the partner in charge of production, send sales questions to the partner in charge of sales. If you are the outside partner, defer to the inside partner on questions about personnel policies.

Like children who run from mom to dad and back to mom looking for the answer they want, your employees, vendors, and customers will detect overlapping authority and play you against your partner for their own benefit. Be clear about who is in charge of what and do not get tricked into saying yes to what your partner has already said no to.

The most important role to define and respect is "the final word." In the privacy of your partners' meeting, there may be mutual respect and deference or violent shouting and passionate disagreement. Within that meeting, partners may resolve conflicts by voting or persuading or arm wrestling. Ties may be broken by flipping coins or playing rock-paper-scissors. The process, however, should be behind closed doors.

In the view of outsiders, you may decide to present a united front of consensus or choose to acknowledge differences of opinions among the partners. Either course is fine.

What must be clear to everyone is that in the end there is one person from whom the final word comes. Otherwise, disagreements will eventually tear the business apart.

Organizations are viewed as hierarchies, no matter how you describe them, and in any business that is larger than just the partners themselves, you will need to define this hierarchy or risk having it done for you by others.

Your hierarchy does not need to diminish the role of any partner or create a reporting relationship between partners. It does not have to change the fact that the partners may make every decision together and by consensus. It only needs to define for others to whom they can look for the final word. A title is the easiest way to indicate who has this authority, but it can also be done by having one partner consistently communicate the partners' decisions.

> **Titles**
>
> Assigning titles to partners can be a bit like arguing about who is going to be the president and vice president of the neighborhood clubhouse. Do not put off the issue with an oxymoron like "Co-CEO." (Co–chief executive officer? Who is chief among the co-chiefs?) If a traditional reporting hierarchy (president, vice president) is not appropriate, use "outside the tree" titles like principal, director, or cofounder.

All Partnerships End

You cannot always control how or when your partnership will end, but you can be sure that it will. Even if your partnership survives marriages, divorces, finances, and personalities (an amazing achievement!), death will eventually snatch a partner away.

The best you can do is to set up a plan for the end that minimizes the cost and damage—personal and financial.

There are many ways in which your partnership can end.

The friendly end is when a partner wants or needs to leave the partnership for reasons unrelated to the business.

- A partner needs to move far away to accompany a spouse or care for an aging parent.
- A partner wants to pursue a different career or devote time to a charity or mission.

The tragic end is when a partner is suddenly unable to continue in the partnership for external reasons beyond the partner's control.

- A partner is terminally ill or is hit by a bus while crossing the street.
- A partner is personally bankrupted by outside investments or a costly divorce.

The torturous end is when a partner checks out of the partnership but does not actually end it.

- A partner stops participating in the business or showing up at work but continues to draw salary and expenses from the business.
- A partner insists on being bought out at an unreasonable (or unaffordable) price and holds the operations and growth of the business hostage to his demands.
- Partners have differing and incompatible views of how to advance the business and enter a stalemate where the business languishes.

The horrifying end is when the partner you chose is replaced by the partner you did not (and would not) choose.

- A partner dies and a spouse/child/idiot-nephew inherits the partner's share.

- A partner is divorced and the bitter ex-spouse, who blames you and the business for the failed marriage, is awarded the partner's share in the business. Or worse, half of the partner's share.

Plan for the End at the Start

When a partnership ends (or when you want it to end), the big issues are control and money. Control and money are things people feel very strongly about and are much easier to discuss at the optimistic, amiable start of a partnership than at the possibly sudden or acrimonious end.

> If you cannot come to a good agreement on control and money at the start of a partnership, you should not enter into it. Control and money are ongoing issues in the life of any partnership, so if you cannot agree on them at the start, you are just setting yourself up for more trouble in the future.

Your plan for the end of the partnership should address a number of issues

- **What events will force the end of the partnership?** Will death, divorce, relocation, or disability force an end of the partnership?
- **Is the partnership more than a shareholding?** Can partners sell their equity in the company to just anyone? Under what conditions? Can it be inherited, or will death force a sale to the other partners?
- **How will irreconcilable differences of opinion be addressed?** Who will have the final say in the partnership? Will there be external arbitration?
- **Who can force the end of the partnership?** Can one partner force the other partner to sell or leave?

- **How will the business be valued?** If a partner needs to be bought out or the business needs to be sold, how will it be valued?
- **How will a buyout be funded?** Where will the funds come from to fund a buyout of a partner (or a partner's surviving spouse or heir)?

Take the time to discuss these issues with your partners and come to an agreement. It is much easier and a whole lot less expensive to do it at the start rather than the end of the partnership. To leave these questions unaddressed is to risk your entire investment in the business.

The Partnership Toolbox

Once you have answers to the key questions about the nature of your partnership and how it will end, you should invest in an attorney's time to draw up the agreement. The good news about structuring a partnership is that it has been done many times before and that lots of great tools are available. (The bad news is that so many partnerships are begun without consulting the toolbox.) Your attorney can explain which standard agreements and clauses will meet your goals and are appropriate for your jurisdiction. Some of the items in the toolbox include the following.

- **Shotgun agreements.** A shotgun agreement is a form of buy-sell agreement in which any partner can "pull the trigger" by making an offer to buy the other partners' shares for a named price. The other partners have a limited time period during which they have the option of reversing the deal and buying the triggering partner's shares for the offered price.

  In the ideal situation, this type of agreement encourages a fair offer. It is open to manipulation, though, if the partners do not have equal access to the funds required to make the purchase or if they have differing interests in continuing in the business.

- **Insurance.** In the early stages of a business, the funds to buy out a partner may not be available to the business or to the other partners. But if a partner dies, the other partners might wish to acquire that partner's shares, rather than taking on a spouse or heir as a partner. Similarly, a partner who is unexpectedly disabled might prefer liquidity to continued shareholding. You can purchase key-man and disability insurance where the business or other partner is the beneficiary and enter into a cross-purchase agreement that forces the purchase of shares with those funds should the policy be claimed.
- **Arbitration.** Include a locally appropriate mechanism for arbitration in any agreement. Valuation, in particular, is very difficult and subjective for privately held businesses and partnerships, and you should anticipate disputes and provide for a resolution mechanism that is less troublesome than going straight to the courts.

Conclusion

Partners usually work together because they share common interests and goals. Over time people change and their interests and goals may go in different directions.

Some people enter perfect partnerships that last for decades to mutual profit and pleasure. Some people win the lottery. It is nice to be one of those people, but it is a bad idea to build your plans around it.

5 Don't Hire Anyone You Haven't Interviewed

When your business is small, hiring new employees can be pretty exciting.

Increased headcount reflects growth in your business. It means that there will be another person to help get all the work done. And, until you make the hire, there is the possibility that you are going to find someone better than perfect: a trilingual twenty-five-year-old with thirty years of experience, two Ph.D.'s, a personal relationship with everyone on your customer prospect list, and who doesn't mind cleaning up the company kitchen in his or her spare time.

The ugly reality of hiring is that it is a huge pain. You have to

- **write the job description.** This can be difficult since you can't just say what you really want to say: "The ideal candidate will help us stop drowning in work!" Job descriptions have to be tight enough to keep everyone from applying, loose enough to attract a variety of applicants, and flexible enough that they don't constrain your relationship with the employee in the future. Oh, and one more thing: they have to be legally compliant, or they will come back at you like razor-edged boomerangs.
- **answer a lot of inquiries.** If you advertise the wage, you risk not hearing from some great candidates or attracting even

more of the not-so-great ones. If you don't advertise the wage, you get a lot of calls that go, "How much does this job pay? . . . Thanks. <click!>" (At least they are efficient.)

- **interview a lot of people.** Interviewing can be a lot of fun, but when you are already so busy that you need to hire more help, do you really have the time for long, casual conversations with strangers who aren't going to become customers? You are too busy for lots of interviews.

It is easy to do a sloppy job of hiring. It is even easier to delegate the job to someone else. Don't do it! Few things are more important to the future success of your business than hiring well. Do not hire anyone you have not interviewed and approved personally. It is worth the time.

Trust me, I know.

How Not to Hire

In the first few years of my business, when we were growing at a breakneck pace, I developed two techniques to keep from being overwhelmed by the hassles of continual hiring.

Bad Idea #1. I let one of our first employees hire most of the other employees. He had more experience with the process than I did. He was willing to do all the work of finding, interviewing, and hiring. He was incredibly patient and detail oriented. He hired lots of great people. He also hired some people who, in retrospect, might have been better suited to different positions. Or positions in different companies. Or in different cities.

Bad Idea #2. When, for whatever reason, I hired people on my own, I hired in the quickest, easiest way possible. I told myself I was just giving everyone a chance, but I was really just lazy and impatient.

- I needed a computer programmer. I called a friend at a larger software company for advice. He told me of an unemployed acquaintance whom his company had recently decided not to hire. "He wasn't good enough for us, but maybe he would be okay for you." I hired him. It was convenient.
- A friend brought another friend by because he needed a job. I did not have an opening at the time, but I made one and hired the guy anyway because we were growing quickly. And he needed a job.
- I hired a summer intern I knew nothing about because he was the college roommate of the intern I had already planned to hire.
- I hired a radio disc jockey because his father (our real estate agent) said he needed a better job.

The amazing thing is that some of these people worked out very well; one has been with us for more than a decade. But if an occasional success validated a fundamentally bad idea, then Russian roulette would be a great party game.

The Trouble Begins

It was not long before personnel problems were a major part of my workload. There was . . .

- **the guy who rarely bathed.** Since this was not enough to *fully* repulse his coworkers, he constantly took and chewed on their pens; this habit was put to rest when one employee rubbed all of his own pens with habanero peppers and awaited their inevitable theft and mastication.
- **the antilearner.** He was cheerful, diligent, reliable, and completely uninterested in learning anything new. "I'd like

you to try this new process/technology/book that could make you twice as efficient," I would suggest. "No thanks. I'll keep doing it this way." (Big smile.) No exceptions: no learning, no growth.

- **the woman who dressed inappropriately.** Yes, we had a dress code. And yes, she was within it. But she . . . just . . . wasn't . . . dressed . . . right . . . in a way you couldn't point out but which couldn't be ignored.
- **the connoisseur of the obscure.** The inquisitive doppelgänger of the antilearner, he was only happy with the most convoluted, awkward, nonstandard way of doing something. Need a copy of the file? It is in a word processing format no one else uses. Would a hammer do the job? Let's use a discontinued water-powered German nail-driving device that requires rechargeable cartridges only available from a Thai distributor.
- **the lazy person.** There is not much to say about those who are lazy. Everybody knows the lazy people. The difference is that I hired the lazy people.
- **the person who never wanted the job.** More than a few people got hired who, it turned out, never wanted the job. They took it because they were desperate, or tired of looking, or who knows why. But they were not happy from day one, and on day one they started making sure no one around them was happy either.

We were approaching one hundred employees. The majority had been hired without any involvement by me; the ones whom I had hired had been hired quickly and with very little thought. Life in the office was one problem after another, and most of the problems involved the same employees again and again.

"Where did these people come from?" I whined at home.

"Well, you hired them," my wife said.

And she was right. The business was staffed with people we had offered jobs to. They had not inherited their jobs. They did not just mysteriously appear at their desks. They were not assigned to us by a government agency. We had actually entered into an agreement to pay these difficult and ineffective employees money to come into our office each day and waste our resources, agitate their coworkers, and grouse at the watercooler.

Why? Because I was willing to invest a week in researching a new technology but would not invest even ten minutes in hiring the right person for the job.

Fixing the Process

I had read lots of business articles and books extolling the importance of hiring the right people. I had read about the large investments companies made in recruiting and interviewing. I had thought all of that was a high-minded luxury of big companies with huge human resources departments.

It occurred to me, at long last, that maybe it wasn't.

Maybe getting the right people was more important than technology or design or market share. Maybe the right people take care of all those things. Maybe the wrong people don't just do their jobs poorly; they weigh down the whole organization and keep the right people from doing their jobs well too. Maybe hiring was not a waste of time. Maybe hiring was the most important thing we were doing.

In the months following my much-delayed recognition of this fundamental business concept, we made a lot of changes. We finally took hiring seriously, and we learned how to do it well.

How to Hire Well

Nothing communicates importance like the personal involvement of the boss. When you are involved in every hire, you are communicating to the existing employees and the future ones that the position is important and that you want to make sure it is filled by the right person.

I do not interview every applicant for every position. I do interview the top few candidates after the manager with the position to fill has identified them. No one is hired that I have not interviewed.

As an organization we have changed the focus of our interviewing from identifying someone who can do the job to identifying someone who wants to do the job and wants to do it well. While certain positions require specific experience, training, or skill, success in most roles in our company comes from attitude and sense. People who are smart, sensible, and want to do a good job work out well. You can teach systems and train for skills. It is a lot harder to teach someone how to have a good attitude or common sense.

> **Know the Law**
>
> Understanding and complying with employment law is essential for everyone involved in hiring for your business. Don't let anyone conduct an interview without training in what is and is not appropriate to ask or say. As the final interviewer and hire/no-hire decision maker, you need to be especially sensitive to your own weak spots. Have your attorney explain potential trouble areas for your type of business. Be on guard for any personal prejudice that could get you into legal trouble or even just deny you a great candidate. (It is not illegal to discriminate against redheads or opera fans, but it would be a waste to do so.)

Don't Hire "Needs the Job" When You Can Hire "Wants the Job"

The first question I ask everyone I interview is the most important one: Why did you apply for this job?

"Mom said I need to get a job and move out," "I heard you have better benefits than my current job," and "It's indoor work" are all wonderful answers because they are huge time-savers. There is no need for a lengthy interview.* After a few second-chance questions, to make sure they weren't just being funny, I can thank them for their time and move on to the next candidate.

We hire people who answer:

- "I use your product, and I really like it. It would be great to be part of the team that makes and sells it."
- "I am really interested in the technology/tools you use, and I want to learn more about them."
- "I want to join a growing company where I will have room for advancement."
- "This job will let me exercise my talent in . . ."
- "I researched your company, and it is a perfect fit for me because . . ."

Leave Room for Surprises

One of the few good side effects of the sloppy hiring practices of our corporate youth was that we stumbled upon some fantastic people who were total surprises. Our indiscriminate hiring picked up people with horrible résumés, or no résumé at all, who turned out to be fantastic employees.

I worry that the better processes we have in place now, which are designed to filter out people who would not fit well, are also filtering out the people who would fit very well but who have no education or experience that would indicate it.

---

*These are all legitimate reasons to apply for a job. As one of many reasons for applying for a specific job, they are each just fine. As the stand-alone answer to the interviewer's question, they indicate a lack of good sense.

To combat this we use two techniques:

- **We put a high value on internal referrals.** A recommendation from an existing employee carries a lot of weight in our hiring process and can put someone with no relevant experience at the top of the list.
- **We let attitude earn a chance.** A great cover letter or an enthusiastic phone call earns consideration (and often a job) for applicants who may not look qualified on paper.

When we hire on this basis, we are clear in the job offer that we see it as a risk for both us and the candidate. If it does not work out, we will be quick to make a change. More often than not, though, these risks pay off, and it is from these successes that we get some of our most exceptional employees.

Take All the Time in the World

If you think hiring the right person takes a lot of time, try hiring the wrong person. Now *that* wastes a lot of time.

I never hired far in advance of our need. If we were hiring to fill an empty position, then the need was usually immediate—we might have only two weeks' notice that someone was leaving. If we were filling a new position, we had probably resisted creating it—and the accompanying increase in payroll—until the need was severe.

In most cases, by the time we were interviewing applicants, we were in a big hurry to fill the position. This created a lot of pressure to hire the best of the applicants rather than the right person for the job.

The best of the applicants is your enemy. The best of the applicants is a siren calling you toward the rocky shoal. "I am the best of the applicants. You need to fill the position. You do not have any more résumés to look at; you do not have time for any more interviews. Hire me; I can start Monday."

Plug your ears. Keep looking.

Sales Is Different

You can't hire salespeople in the same way you hire everyone else; a résumé means less when hiring for a sales job. Some of our best salespeople had no sales experience. Some people with great sales experience could not sell our product. Sales performance is easy to quantify—you either hit the numbers or not—so sales is the job where everyone gets a chance.

Maybe you cannot find or even identify the *perfect* candidate. Maybe you will have to train for a few specific skills. Maybe you want to take a chance on someone with a great attitude. That is all fine.

It is okay to hire a candidate who is not perfect.

It is not okay to hire a candidate who is simply convenient.

How do you know which candidate is right and which is simply convenient? There isn't one answer; sometimes the right candidate is an obvious star, and sometimes that person is harder to identify. Look at your own motives for wanting to say yes to a candidate. Ask yourself, "Am I compromising and simply choosing the best of the candidates I have seen?" If so, don't.

All Hiring Processes Can Fail

For every business there is a different recruiting and interviewing process that works best. Detailed examinations on technical skill might be essential for your business while in-depth background checks and character references might be most important for another. Some businesses hire a recruiting firm to run a national search, and others conduct two-day interviews.

Whatever your process is, it can still fail. No matter how much time you invest in recruiting and hiring, you can still end up hiring the wrong person.

When trouble appears, nip it in the bud. Fire someone *today.* It is

Keeping It in the Family

I often describe my company as a family business. It is true that I have several of my family members working with me, but there is more to it than that. We have a lot of other families working with us too. A quarter of our employees have a brother, sister, spouse, parent, child, or cousin working in the company.

Many of the characteristics of good or exceptional employees are common to others in their family. An employee with strong values, a good work ethic, and a positive attitude is likely to have family members with similar virtues. And family members are usually the best qualified to give honest recommendations; it is in their personal and professional interest to correctly encourage or discourage the hiring of a relative. (To avoid nepotism we do not let family members hire or directly supervise each other.)

There are some obvious problems that come from hiring multiple people from one family. We have lost good employees in pairs when a family relocated, and there have been rare and awkward occasions when one member of a family was fired. The overall experience has been positive, though, and we still try to hire family members of good employees whenever we can.

embarrassing to admit to such a big mistake quickly, but the embarrassment is ultimately less painful than continuing the mistake and allowing the wrong person to become more deeply integrated into your organization.

The Wisest Investment

Hiring the wrong people wastes your time, drains your resources, and demoralizes your team. Hiring the wrong people increases the likelihood of employment claims and lawsuits. Hiring the wrong people does not save any time; you will eventually need to hire the right people in order to grow your business—if it survives the wrong people.

Learn how to recruit and identify the best candidates. Plan ahead and invest as much time as necessary in filling every position with the right person. Be personally involved in interviewing.

Hiring well is the wisest investment you can make in your business.

My friend Adam is the CEO of a high-tech company. With his vice president of sales, he hired an aggressive new salesperson for a travel-heavy position. On the new salesperson's first day of work, he reported to the VP of sales. His new boss handed him a portable e-mail device that all the company salespeople use on the road.

"I don't need that," said the new salesperson.

"Yes, you do," replied the VP of sales. "We need you to be in e-mail contact with the office and clients while you are traveling."

"No, I don't need that," said the new salesperson.

When the VP of sales called Adam, he got the right advice: "If you can't stand him on the first day of work, fire him now." He did.

6 Cash Is King

If there were a book of business poetry, it would be full of odes to cash.

Cash is the only life-and-death issue for your business. There are lots of important things you can worry about—people, products, service—but they are important because they impact cash. Businesses with cash live. Businesses without cash die.

Profit is important, and it is the reason businesses exist, but it is not more important than cash. If you have the cash, you can run an unprofitable company for years. Many companies in fields like bioscience have long research and development cycles and have yet to sell a product. A number of dot-com companies still in business today have never earned a profit. They are all in business because they have cash in the bank.

> **Cash Is Not a Number**
>
> Do not confuse cash with income or expenses. Your receivables might slow down or even disappear if a customer is experiencing their own cash crisis. You may be able to get extended terms or use a rolling reserve against returns to defer cash payments on payables. Cash is a precious substance, not a piece of data.

Enron was one of the most spectacular business failures on record. Arrogance, greed, and corruption are among the many reasons given for its demise. The reason for the actual failure, though, was that they ran out of cash. As long as they had cash (and could continue to get more), the doors stayed open and the lights stayed on. Moral and ethical failings may have led to it, but the collapse did not come until the day the cash was gone.

Cash Is About Survival

Cash equals survival—for your business and for you. Unless you are running a restaurant, cash is the only thing in your business that you can eat.*

There was a time when I could not cash my own paycheck because the business was out of cash. The business was already pretty large and had been profitable for years. It had significant assets, staff, and inventory and was even in the process of getting new equity investment. It was just really tight on cash. In the big picture we were doing all right, so I wasn't worried. I saw it as a temporary inconvenience. When I found my personal bank account empty on a Friday afternoon at the grocery store, though, I learned this embarrassing lesson: you can have a car, a house, and a profitable business, but without cash you cannot eat.

Valuable Business Assets	Directly Exchangeable for Food
Customers	No
Employees	No
Inventory	No
Profits	No
Cash	Yes

*If you are running a restaurant, it can still be bad. When my wife was young, her family ran a restaurant that failed. They ate frozen crab legs for weeks afterward—and today my wife is allergic to crab.

There is no way to predict the extraordinary expenses that come up in business—having cash on hand is the best way to prevent these bumps from derailing your train.

My business licenses electronic rights to books and databases. In the process of acquiring rights to a new title, we discovered that we had accidentally left a previously licensed title from the same publisher off of our royalty calculation spreadsheets for more than five years. The accrued royalties were significant. Having cash on hand, though, allowed us to survive the crisis. We were able to make a single payment to catch up and to preserve the relationship. We also avoided a license revocation that could have forced us to reconfigure our products, destroy inventory, and incur even more expenses.

Cash Is About Opportunity

The real power of cash is that it creates opportunities. When you have cash, you can move more quickly than your competition. You can exploit opportunities before anyone else, and you can create new opportunities by putting your cash to work.

I once had a smaller competitor that was a profitable division of a public company that was in big trouble. The public company needed to focus on its core business and was willing to sell my competitor to me. It was the perfect acquisition: I would acquire a profitable product line and a solid base of repeat customers that could be moved easily to my platform while reducing the overall overhead. The price was great too because the public company was desperate for cash.

I did not have the cash, though, or the time to arrange financing. The seller was in a hurry and gave the division to a large creditor in exchange for release from the debt. Today, I keep enough cash on hand to do that deal, or one like it, if it comes up again.

Cash Gets Great Discounts

Your accountant can help determine if you should take a 2% cash discount from a vendor or pay Net 30. That's peanuts, though. You should be looking for opportunities to save 30–50% (or more!) by slapping cash on the barrelhead.

Looking for big discounts is not about exploiting others' weaknesses. It is about understanding that cash can be worth more than its monetary value and that everybody has a different cost to acquire it. Your early, discounted cash payment could be the difference between meeting payroll or not for a vendor. A great discount for you could be cheaper than the outrageous rate at which a vendor has financed its receivables while still being more than you could earn on the cash yourself.

My last house was new construction covered with a guaranteed siding material. It was discovered that a manufacturing defect caused this siding to rot away in just a few years. The manufacturer was buried with warranty claims, and soon homeowners were buried, too, with piles of time-consuming paperwork related to a class action lawsuit.

My claim under the class action was approved and a payment specified. The only problem was that the payment would not be made for years—and only then if the company chose to refund the already tapped-out claims fund.

A planned move of my business to a new city meant that I had to replace the siding immediately in order to sell the house. All my cash was going into these repairs and the purchase of the new home, and all my borrowing power was going into the new mortgage.

When a letter arrived with a check offering a heavily discounted early payment in exchange for release from the claim, I cashed it immediately. It was a welcome relief from the hassles and uncertainty of the ongoing claim and provided cash at a time when I could really use it. Financially it was a terrible deal, but it removed the risk and provided cash I had no other way to acquire.

I learned later that this discounted payment plan allowed the company to settle $91 million in claims for $32 million in cash. That is the power of cash!

Managing Your Cash

The way cash flows and how much you need to have on hand is different for every business. The need to manage it well—to respect and even love it—is universal.

Your bank can help you manage your cash with tools like lockboxes and sweep accounts. They will know which tools are the best fit for your business.

Securing a line of credit when you do not need one, for the day when you do, is another way you can build a cash safety net.

The most important part of cash management, though, is in your hands. You need to create a cash-aware company culture and, unless you are more disciplined than any entrepreneur I have met, put systems in place to protect you from yourself.

When cash is tight, you need systems to ration it while doing as little damage as possible to your business and reputation. Here are some of the things you can do to ration cash.

- **Slow down your payables.** Call your vendors and be honest with them. Tell them things are tight and when they're going to get better. Apologize and ask for longer terms. Make partial payments even if they are not required. It shows good faith and puts off worries that you won't meet your obligations.
- **Create an expense review committee.** People hate committees. They're big and slow and terrible at making decisions. That is why you should create a committee to review and preapprove every expense over one-hundred dollars. Put your most tightfisted staff on it, and do not sign any check the committee has not approved. (Make sure the committee meets as infrequently as possible.)
- **Don't pay the rent.** Unless you are in a very hot market for commercial real estate, no one is more interested in your

continued success than your landlord. It is difficult, expensive, and time consuming to evict a tenant, and there may be a lot of vacant months before a new tenant starts paying rent. The landlord knows this. When things are tight, call the landlord and be completely honest.

When cash is plentiful, good decisions are more difficult. You need to find balance between hoarding it for safety and employing it to grow and seize opportunities.

In my business we maintain four levels of cash.

- **The top level is the working cash.** This is the money we use on a daily basis to run the company, and the balance of this account is watched carefully every day. We are careful with this cash but not afraid to use it.

- **The next level is the working cash reserves.** Every day we set aside a percentage of that day's sales to cover large, regular expenses. By reserving the cash for payroll, taxes, and other fixed-percentage costs ahead of time, we ensure that we'll *never* miss a payment on the most important payables. (This also prevents us from having misleadingly large amounts of working cash available just before large quarterly payments are due. If we did not set aside the cash for these expenses, our management team could be making decisions based on bad data—spending money that we would need the next week.)

- **Level three is the rainy-day reserves.** This is where we accumulate cash for surprise threats and opportunities—an acquisition, capital expenses, dispute settlements, etc. We do not touch this cash without approval from me and several senior managers. If possible we do not touch it at all—we try to cover these expenses from the working cash.

- **The bottom level of our cash reserves is the squirrel fund—acorns saved for winter.** We set it up when we came out of a period of heavy debt and had a product that was a surprise bestseller. We took a portion of the excess cash it generated and took it to a new bank where we put it in an account with only one signer. The banker was surprised when we declined the checkbook for the account. To use those funds, I have to go to the bank in person and fill out a bunch of paperwork. I wish it was even less convenient than that.

> Every morning you should know how much cash your business has on hand. You should know how much you will have for the next week, have a good idea how much you will have for the next month, and have a plan for how much you will have for the next year.

A friend has a specialty construction business that involves large customer deposits against costs that can stretch out over two years. She has identified the danger of spending those deposits on operational expenses and getting caught without the funds to cover the materials expenses that follow a year or more later. To avoid a crisis, she has set up a cash management procedure that keeps deposits apart from operating cash, trickling out funds in careful relation to project costs.

Your business has unique needs. Find the most paranoid, conservative cash management system you can that meets them.

Cash is safety; cash is opportunity; cash is power. Cash is king.

7 Quality, Price, Service—Prioritize

I was blessed with immediate success in my software company. We had the right product at the right time, and our start-up was profitable in the first year. A few years of 100% growth convinced me that I was a business genius.

As a self-designated business genius, I was convinced that we could dominate our category while setting new standards for excellence in every area. We were going to have fantastic products, we were going to offer excellent customer service, and we were going to offer the best value.

Being the best meant committing the necessary resources. We hired programmers and testers to help improve the quality of the software. We upgraded our phone system to handle all the lines necessary for our expanded customer service and technical support departments. We offered packaged software for as little as $9.95 and had a configuration just below every competitor's price point.

The increase in infrastructure was timed perfectly to coincide with a slowdown in our sales. The market window that had enabled our rapid growth was closing; the competition was catching up. At a time when we needed to focus, we were instead burning huge amounts of cash in an attempt to be the best in every way.

The QPS Triangle

My friend Tony was familiar with our business and was concerned about our spending and lack of focus. Tony sat me down in his office and pulled out a legal pad. On the pad he drew a triangle:

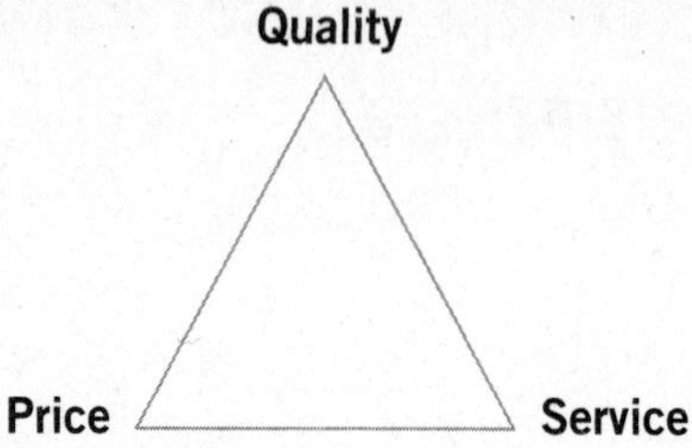

Tony explained that the triangle represented my business and that its three corners were the three characteristics on which the business could compete. He explained how the three characteristics are in tension: given an extra dollar I could choose to spend it on improving quality, offering better service, or reducing prices, but not all three.

He asked me to put a mark in the triangle that represented my company's emphasis. Believing that all three characteristics were equally important, I put the mark right in the center. If I'd had an extra dollar, I'd have put thirty-three cents into becoming more competitive on all three fronts. I was unwilling to give on any point.

That mark correctly described my business, but as Tony explained to me, it was the reason I was so dizzy. The business was spinning in circles.

The Emphasis Arrow

Where you place your emphasis within the triangle determines the direction and momentum of your business. Imagine an arrow that starts at the center of the triangle and goes to your emphasis mark. The direction of the arrow is the direction you are pushing your business triangle. The length of the arrow represents the momentum of your business as it moves in the direction of the arrow.

Placing your emphasis anywhere but the center represents an emphasis on one characteristic at the expense of others—but it gives you direction. Trying to emphasize the center sets your business spinning in circles.

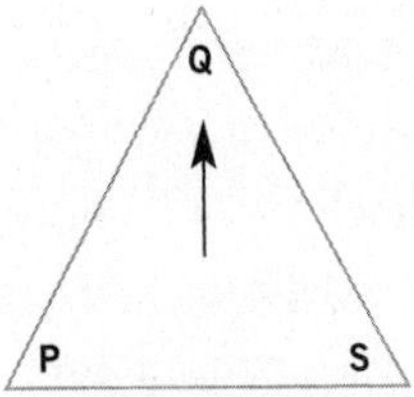

Focused on Quality
Strong Momentum

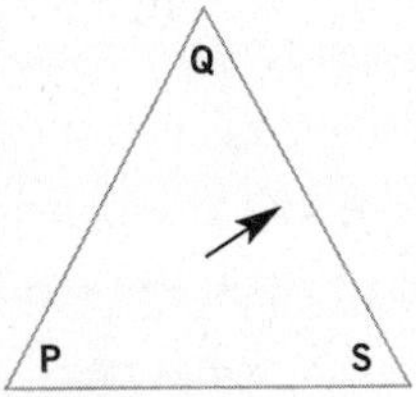

Quality and Service
Some Momentum

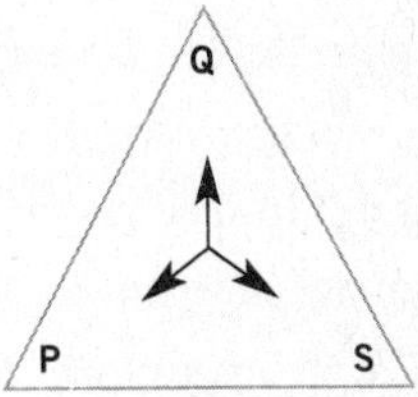

All Three
Spinning in Circles

Choosing an emphasis for your company does not mean you can simply ignore the unemphasized characteristics. Exceptional quality or service may earn a higher price, but not a limitless one. And no price is low enough to counter a complete lack of quality or service. The emphasis simply points in the direction of your priorities.

- **Pointing at a corner** means you can focus on just one thing.
- **Pointing at a side** means you need to constantly balance your two goals.
- **Sitting in the center** means you are spinning in circles.

Choosing Your Emphasis

The great thing about the QPS Triangle is that you can be successful with a mark anywhere in it. (You can even be successful with a mark in the center, though it is difficult.) The key is putting your emphasis mark far away from the marks of your competitors.

The easiest place to put your emphasis is in an empty corner. If your competitor is hanging a sign that reads, "We'll Beat Any Price," you should take a look at the quality and service corners. If your market is full of expensive premium products, you should be investigating low-price alternatives.

Most businesses put their emphasis along one side of the triangle. They have a primary emphasis and a secondary one that is close behind. This works, especially when the competition is somewhere else in the triangle, but it results in a shorter arrow and less momentum.

Target is a good example of a chain that has positioned itself on a side. In recent years it has moved along the price-quality side, toward quality, without a significant change in service. By redefining itself as "high quality at great prices," it has distinguished itself from competitors and removed pressure to compete head-to-head.

Kmart would be an example of a "spinner." For years it offered a confusing message and lacked a distinct role in the market as it tried to compete in every corner.

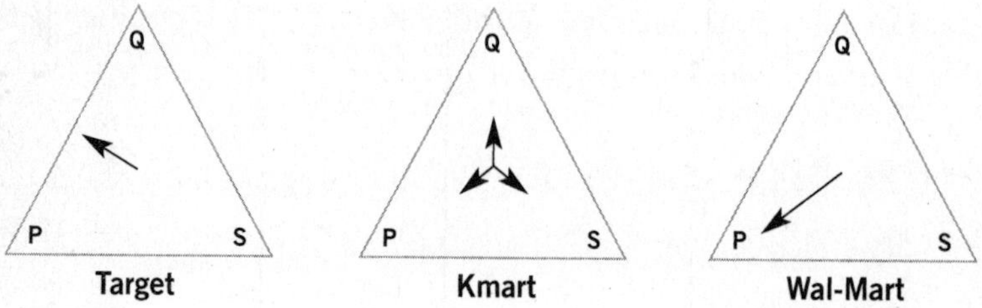

Moving deep into one corner is a powerful strategy that creates the longest arrow and the most momentum. The focus on a single corner makes decision making easy, and it usually puts a lot of distance between you and your competitors.

Wal-Mart is an example of both the distance and momentum that come from such single-minded focus.

The Wal-Mart motto, "Always Low Prices. Always." is a clear positioning statement that sets Wal-Mart apart from all its competitors in the minds of customers. If I want a good microwave at a reasonable price, there are lots of places I can go. If I want a *really cheap* microwave, I head straight to Wal-Mart.

The Wal-Mart motto is also a guideline for operations. When you are competing only on price, it is easier to make decisions. You just take the low-cost option and move on.

Scenario	Decision Making at Target	Decision Making at Wal-Mart
Store Location	Find middle ground between expensive locations at the center of town and cheaper locations farther out.	It is cheaper on the edge of town.
New Teapot	Hire an architect to design a teapot that looks great but is still reasonably priced.	Buy a boatload of cheap teapots. Offer to buy two boatloads for a bigger discount.
Fashion	Balance style and cost. Hire models. Get celebrities to wear Target clothes during TV appearances.	Save money by having employees model house-brand clothes in advertisements.

When you are deep in one corner of the triangle, you get momentum from the focus both inside and outside your organization. It is easier for you to act quickly when you know exactly what you are about. It is easy to put aside distractions and resource drains when you are committed to competing in just one way. It is also easier for customers to think about you. On an edge of the triangle there is usually less distance to a competitor. Customers need to choose between the way your business and your competitors have balanced strengths. Businesses deep in the corner get to own one of the three primary characteristics in the minds of customers. This makes it easier for customers to choose you and leads to faster growth.

Expanding the Triangle

In well-established markets, it is likely that all three corners are already occupied by strong companies. You may find the center filled in as well.

In this case you need to expand the triangle. Expanding the triangle shortens all your competitors' momentum lines. It redefines today's corners as part of the center, and it creates room for you anywhere you would like, in a corner or on the sides.

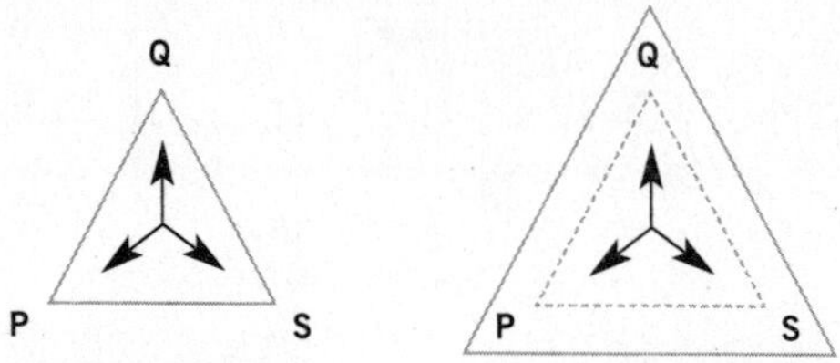

Original Triangle
No Room for Distinction

Expanded Triangle
Room to Compete

To expand the triangle, you simply need to stake out a position that is beyond what anyone is doing in your market today. If you want to compete on price in a market where a competitor already fills that corner, you need to find a way to offer customers an even lower priced proposition. To expand the triangle with quality or service, you need to define a whole new level of quality or service.

Internet grocery services grew the triangle by pushing service. For an extra fee you can have someone walk your shopping list through a store, squeezing the produce to your specifications. They then deliver the groceries to your door—or even right into your refrigerator.

Pushing the boundary on any part of the triangle makes the whole triangle bigger because it expands people's perceptions of what is acceptable or normal in the market. When a market triangle is filled, everyone understands the balance of trade-offs in each corner; there is an implicit baseline for price in the quality and service corners, for quality in the price and service corners, etc. There is also an implicit maximum benefit: a lowest price, a best quality, or service.

In cellular phones, Vertu pushed the limits on quality with a $20,000 handset that features precious metals and a sapphire crystal display. Hop-on.com stripped quality and service to a minimum and removed the display entirely in order to create a forty-dollar disposable device. Both companies expanded the triangle by pushing their respective corners farther out. They also redefined baseline expectations for the opposite corners: before Vertu, no phone could be of high enough quality to warrant a $20,000 price tag; before Hop-on.com, a display was a minimum requirement for a cell phone.

You expand the triangle by setting a new maximum value in one corner (or along a side). In most cases you will also have to define a new baseline for the other corners. You will need to offer even less service or quality in order to support the new low price, or you will need to charge a higher price than ever before to support your quality or service.

Warehouse stores expanded the triangle for groceries by pushing the price to new lows in exchange for dramatically reduced quality and service. They have less-convenient locations, only one brand of mayonnaise in only one size container, and customers select most items right off the pallets they arrived on.

Make Your Mark and Stick to It

Soon after Tony showed me the triangle, I went to a dinner where Jeffrey Brotman, founder of Costco, was speaking on his experience building that chain of warehouse stores. He started by giving the answer to the question he hears most often: Why doesn't Costco open express lanes and make it easier to run in for a few items quickly?

Brotman explained that Costco built a business around the best possible prices on quality merchandise. The trade-off for those prices is reduced selection and convenience and higher-volume transactions. He doesn't want someone using a parking space, clogging an aisle, and ringing up a transaction just to buy a carton of milk—even a huge carton of milk. Those low prices come at the cost of some convenience: Costco shoppers know parking is tough, they'll have to show a card to get in, and there is going to be a line at checkout. That is why Costco shoppers make an event out of visiting the store, holding off on some purchases for a week or longer so they can get everything on one trip.

I realized that Costco had put a mark on the price-quality side of the triangle and was quite consciously sacrificing service in order to offer more value on the chosen side. I saw how their focus gave them momentum and clarity of purpose. And I found the rallying cry that turned my own company around.

"Costco doesn't want me crowding their store or using a parking space unless I have $150 worth of stuff in my cart," I announced at the office. "And I don't want us answering the phone except to support a $150 product."

Software can be complex and intimidating. Our users told us that they want good, patient support. It is important to me to deliver a quality product. So we put a mark on the service-quality side of the triangle and said good-bye to low prices. In the following months we systematically eliminated all of our base products with prices below $150. We turned down a number of opportunities for wide distribution of a low-priced configuration. We weighed all of our strategic decisions against our chosen position in the market.

The result was fewer customers—but better customers. The customers we retained were the serious users of our software, not the people who picked it up off a discount rack. And they were profitable. We were able to offer them better support even while reducing our support costs. We were able to invest in building higher-quality software instead of churning out lots of cheap new packages. Our spinning company stopped spinning and started moving in one direction. We returned from breaking even to being profitable again.

8 Nobody Needs an Optimistic Accountant

You should be optimistic about your business. Your salespeople should be optimistic about your business. Your parents, your children, your vendors, and your employees should be optimistic about your business. You do not want any negative, pessimistic, whining, crybaby Chicken Littles on your team. Except for your accountant.

Your accountant, controller, bookkeeper, CFO—whoever it is that counts your money—should be a pessimist. Your accountant should not be the kind of person who thinks things are always going to get better. Your accountant should be the kind of person who thinks things are always going to get worse. Your accountant should be the kind of person who, when you say, "Good morning," responds, "We'll see."

In your business the two people with the best intuitive feel for the numbers, and thus for the overall health of the business, are you and your accountant. (If that is not true for your business, it should be.) As the leader of your business, it is your job to be optimistic about the numbers. You should be looking for ways to stretch and grow your business, to make forward-looking investments, and to take the big risks that offer big rewards.

A business does not have to be very large before the numbers get complex and misleading. Today's cash balance may be easy to find out, but predicting the numbers a month or more in the future can be difficult. Is this customer really going to pay on time? What will be the true cost of that project? Which bill is going to come, and which sale is going to close?

If your accountant has the same optimistic, go-getter attitude as you do, there will be no one who is well-informed enough about the financial state of the business to persuasively argue with you. You need someone to temper your enthusiasm and stop you from making moves that are too risky. Since you cannot be the voice of caution—who wants to follow a pessimistic leader?—you need to make sure you have an accountant who is.

The Dangers of an Optimistic Accountant

One of the most important questions you ask in running your business is "Can we afford this?" It doesn't matter if you are asking the question about a luxury (a staff masseuse), a risky plan for growth (advertising, new hires, new warehouse), or even necessities (payroll, coffee, toilet paper). You can't afford to incorrectly answer yes to this question very often.

Optimistic people like to answer yes to the question, "Can we afford this?" They like to answer yes to everything. Yes is so much nicer than no, and optimistic people like to be nice. Besides, they are sure that you *can* afford it. Things are going well and will probably get better. And you would not be asking if it was not important, right? So spending the money will only make things better!

Optimistic people really are nice. This is why it is dangerous to have an optimistic person as your accountant.

In the early days of our business, my partners and I were focused on building the product and selling it. We needed someone to watch over the financial side of the business so that we could focus on what we saw as the heart of the operation.

We were excited to find Lisa, a bookkeeper with lots of experience in much larger organizations. Lisa had a great attitude. She enjoyed her work, was enthusiastic about our business, and believed, along with us, that the company was right on the edge of a major growth phase.

The business was chaotic. Large sums of money were going in and out every day. After struggling to keep track of everything ourselves, working with Lisa was a refreshing change.

Lisa jumped right in and started helping us build our infrastructure, establish better systems, and grow the business. Because we had not yet developed the internal financial reports we should have, we counted on Lisa to tell us how we were doing. We would ask her about sales, profitability, and available cash. Most importantly, we would not invest in anything new or make any significant purchases without asking Lisa, "Can we afford this?"

The answer was always yes.

It didn't seem as ridiculous to me then as it seems now. At the time, I actually believed it. Our sales were growing, and we were bringing in outside investment. Business was booming, and the office was buzzing. Lisa was obviously immersed in our finances; surely she knew what we could and could not afford.

It was true: Lisa was immersed in our finances. She was so immersed that she was drowning. The chaos of rapid growth and constant change was not only making it hard to see the financial picture clearly, it was feeding Lisa's naturally optimistic view of the company as a rapidly growing success. She was sure that we could afford to do all the things we wanted to do; and if not, she was sure that by tomorrow we would be able to. She didn't want to be the one to hold us back. She didn't want to be the one to say no to obviously important investments. So she said yes and worked extra hours to find ways to make things work out.

Some of the ways in which Lisa made things work out included stretching payments in order to keep more cash in the bank—at first within terms and soon long beyond. When the payables numbers started to look bad, she found ways to massage things by slowing down the interaction between the accounting system and the mail. Inbound bills took longer to get opened and entered into the system; outbound checks took longer to get from the check printer to the mailbox.

In another display of optimism, bad receivables were never written off and late collections never anticipated. The working assumption was that receivables would come in on time and that they would all come in, no matter how old or unlikely they were to be paid. This also helped to support the mistaken belief that the business was in acceptable financial health.

Lisa was even optimistic about the financial tools we needed; for more than a year, she was always just a week or two from having the daily reporting system ready.

When the house of cards collapsed, Lisa left suddenly. I needed

Signs Your Accountant Is Too Optimistic

- Keeps asking your salespeople, "What's new and exciting?"
- Your company checks have the smiley-face pattern.
- Says things like, "You've got to spend money to make money."
- Suggests serving prime rib at the corporate Christmas party.

Signs Your Accountant Is on the Right Track

- Constantly fighting salespeople over expense reports.
- The locked cabinet containing your corporate checkbook is rusted shut.
- Says things like, "Are you done with that tea bag? It's good for another cup."
- Suggests serving cocktail weenies at the corporate Christmas party.

emergency help that I could trust, so I brought in an outside accounting firm. They found things like unmailed checks in the backs of drawers and stacks of unpaid bills. Things were a mess. Our financial condition was far worse than we had realized.

As much as I wanted to, I could not blame Lisa. She had not lied. She had not generated false reports. She had not absconded with funds to an island nation with no extradition treaty. Rather, she had worked very hard to keep the corporate ship afloat against a flood of foolish spending and bad decisions. Her only failing was an overeager desire to please and a misplaced optimism.

I was at fault. I had hired the optimistic accountant. I had believed her every time she said yes because it was what I wanted to believe. Besides Lisa and me, there was no one else in the organization who knew enough to sound the alarm, and the two of us were just encouraging each other to believe that things would get better.

What to Do with an Optimistic Accountant

My brother-in-law Andy is the head of our accounting department today. He is a certified public accountant and a very nice guy. This is a good thing on the weekends but a bit of a problem in the office: he can be pretty optimistic.

I wanted Andy to join our business because I had been impressed with his work over the years and because I knew that as a family member and shareholder he would be especially protective of our resources. We just needed to find a way to address his natural optimism.

Over the years, we have worked out some techniques to address this occupational character flaw.

- **We don't let accounting hear fantasy sales projections.** Our best salespeople are incurable optimists. After the first call on a new lead, they are calculating commissions. One salesperson asked for a doubling of inventory based on his hunch after an initial sales contact. Yes, some of the big deals are closed, but rarely as quickly as the salesperson hopes. We keep dramatic sales projections within the sales department unless they are projections for a decrease. In that case, accounting is the first to hear.

- **The accounting department pads its estimates.** The accounting department overestimates expenses and underestimates income in all of its reports and projections. The goal is to be as accurate as possible while ensuring that the final numbers will *never* differ from the estimate in the wrong direction.
- **We control the vocabulary.** The word *if* is considered suspect in statements by members of the accounting department. I don't want to hear things like *if* we close that deal, *if* the sales meet projections, *if* next month is as good as this month, etc. The phrase *in case* is preferred: we have funds set aside *in case* we don't close that deal; we have a plan to cut expenses *in case* sales don't meet projections, etc.
- **I ask, "What would happen if . . . ?"** . . . sales dropped 10% next month? . . . our tax estimate was off? . . . we didn't ship the new product on time? While it would be demoralizing to ask these questions throughout the organization, it is very helpful to ask them of the accountant. It helps reinforce a cautious attitude and often reveals unforeseen liabilities.

Andy and I understand our roles clearly now: I cheer on the team, plan for a brighter tomorrow, and lead the parade. Andy rains on the parade.

Only Your Accountant Will Do

A cautious confidant is a valuable asset. You need someone you can talk to about risks and who can balance your passion with prudence. If you are doing a good job of inspiring your team, they will not be able to help you enough in this area—you will have already poisoned them with enthusiasm. Add to that their natural reluctance to contradict the boss, no matter how friendly you are, and they are simply not up to the task.

Your accountant is the best person for the role of nervous Nellie. Your accountant is uniquely positioned to understand the financial condition of your business and uniquely equipped with data you can't argue with: the numbers.

Best of all, if you do decide to take the safe way, everyone will understand when you blame it on your accountant.

9 You Can Always Find 5%

No matter what my income over the years, I have always felt like things would be okay financially if I earned just 5% more. Even when I have experienced dramatic increases in salary, I have found that my expenses catch up very quickly, bringing me back to the edge of break even.

I have talked with lots of small-business people who also live right on the edge. Their business is in a perpetual cash crunch because their expenses always seem to be right behind (if not a bit ahead of) their income. Five percent is often the difference between losing money and making money.

Now, I understand that lots of individuals and businesses have financial difficulties that make 5% look like pigeon feed. That is a whole other chapter: Chapter 11. I am talking about the businesses that are basically doing all right, but seem to be perpetually treading water to stay at the break-even point. For these businesses 5% is the difference between profit and loss—and that is a big difference.

The good news is that you can always find 5%.

Where to Look for Your 5%

The 5% you're looking for is hiding in one of two places: your expenses or your income. If you are lucky, you have 5% hiding in each place, and you can introduce the 5%'s to each other for a lovely 10% improvement.

Cutting 5% from Your Expenses

The first and best place to look at is what you are spending on. Hack off the big pieces of fat before you get into the delicate trimming.

Your tools for fat hacking are three reports.

- **Expenses by category in descending order.** This high-level report from your accounting software should break things into around thirty expense categories. Ideally you should have real-time access to breakdowns within the categories when using this report.
- **Checks written summed by payee in descending order.** Who is getting your money? The expense report tells you what you are spending on, but not necessarily with whom. Sometimes a vendor is getting paid through a lot of categories. This report helps you see where the money is actually going.
- **Payroll by name in descending order.** Over time it is possible to lose track of what you are actually paying your staff. Raises, commissions, and different hire dates can make it hard to remember the real ranking of employees by cost—or even what their true cost is.

The three reports contain overlapping data, but the different arrangements force you to look at your costs from multiple perspectives.

Generate the reports with data from the trailing twelve months. Monthly data hides seasonal variations, quarterly bills, and special events like bonuses. Monthly data also makes the numbers look too small. Payroll and most expenses are ongoing costs that are not adjusted frequently. Your reports should reflect the size of your annual expense for each line item.

Work through each report line by line and ask the questions:

"What would happen if this number was cut in half? What if it were zero?"

- **Expenses.** If I stopped all spending in this category, what is the worst thing that could happen? What would I lose? Could I live with half of what I am currently getting from this spending?

- **Payees.** If I never wrote another check to this payee, what is the worst thing that could happen? Am I getting this much value from this payee? Is there someone else who could give me the same value for half this amount?

- **Employees.** If these people quit tomorrow, would I replace them? Would I assign their tasks to someone else or just stop having them done? Are the tasks they are doing worth what it is costing me to have them done?

Every time I go through this process, I think it is going to be a waste of time. If there is something so unimportant on the report that it could be cut to zero, why would we have ever started spending on it in the first place?

I am usually surprised, though, to find that there are always a few lines that can be completely eliminated and many others that can be dramatically reduced. The format of the reports also reveals unexpectedly high costs. You may be racking up higher bills in professional services without realizing it, or a commission structure may be flawed (or manipulated) in a way that is dramatically overcompensating one salesperson. Ranking costs in a descending order helps you judge their relative value.

Payroll is likely one of your largest expenses, and that is why it is critical to ask the "what would happen" question about each name on the list. While it is the most unpleasant place to make dramatic cuts, it is also one of the most productive because excess employees are generating costs beyond their salary in space, benefits, equipment, training, overhead, etc.

Looking at the ranked payroll list and using the "what would happen" questions forces you to look at the value that each employee adds to the business. This perspective is different from the normal view where you are evaluating an employee's work and performance. Ultimately it does not matter if employees are smart, capable, and productive if the work they are doing does not add value in excess of their cost to the organization.

Finding 5% in Your Bills

The great thing about 5% is that it is small enough to ignore but big enough to make a difference. The key is being the person who does not ignore it in a world full of people who do.

Five percent of any given bill or invoice usually is not a big deal. Even if it is a big number, it is just one-twentieth of the whole amount. It is only a big deal when it is 5% of *everything.* Any individual supplier you purchase from is not likely to feel a 5% difference in your bill very much. You will, however, feel a 5% difference in the sum total of all your bills.

I once sat in a room full of entrepreneurs who were commiserating about the economy and the state of their businesses. Most of us were seeing slower sales and payments and generally feeling the effects of a cautious and tight economy. There was a lot of grumbling but not much in the way of solutions until my friend Fred told us about The Letter.

Fred has a high-volume, low-margin business that was being squeezed by a slowdown in orders. He felt that in order to compensate for the slower turnover he needed to increase his margin. Raising prices was risky, though, because his products were repeat-order commodities and competitors could use his price increase to lure away customers.

Fred realized that his sales were wide and shallow. He sold a small number of units to a large number of customers. However, his suppliers' sales channels were narrow and deep. There were not many companies that bought as much as Fred's did. His business was worth a lot to the suppliers and would be difficult to replace. And Fred's suppliers sold a commodity product; Fred could easily switch to another supplier.

Fred and his CFO cowrote The Letter to all their suppliers. It pointed out that times were tough and acknowledged that they were probably tough for the supplier too. Nonetheless, Fred's company needed to reduce expenses, and so it would be paying 5% less on all invoices starting the next month. If that is a problem, they concluded, give us a call so we can discuss it.

I was blown away by the audacity of The Letter. Fred was telling his suppliers unilaterally that their prices had to come down and by how much and when. What amazed me even more was that he was getting very little push-back from his suppliers. Most of them were accepting his new terms.

Fred's story inspired me. I did not believe we had the same kind of strength in our relationship with suppliers that Fred had with his, but I realized we could do something similar. When I got back to my office, I called a meeting of our management team. We took a list of our suppliers and went through it name by name and then assigned managers to call them about price reductions.

Within days we reduced our costs by more than 2%, saving thousands each month. Over the next few months, we received even more price reductions. We did not write The Letter. We did not threaten to move our business to a competitor. All we did was ask.

Who to ask. Ultimately you want to ask everyone. You will get the most benefit by reducing your biggest expenses, though, which is why you start at the top of your ranked list of payees. You are most likely to get concessions from suppliers selling commodity products or services in fiercely competitive businesses like telecommunications, printing, and Internet services.

How to ask. Politely. The person who knows best how and how much you can reduce your expenses with a supplier is the supplier. You want to engage them in helping you instead of turning them into an adversary in a negotiation.

Be informed. Before approaching a supplier about cost reductions, you need to do some research. Ask businesses that do not compete with you what they are paying for similar products or services. Get pricing or quotes from their competitors. Ask your supplier's competitors about your supplier. What is their reputation in their industry? Are they the low-cost or high-cost provider?

Search the Internet for background on your supplier. Are they big or small? Are they a healthy business or a hurting one? Does their CEO brag about their high margins in news stories? Get an idea of how important your business is to your supplier and how much room they have to work with.

Have a goal. You should have a savings goal in mind based on your research and your cost-cutting needs. While 5% is a great overall goal, you will find that some costs can be reduced much more and others have only enough margin to allow a tiny cut. Set your goal within the parameters of your research.

Share your problem. I have had the most success in reducing costs when I approached my supplier with my problem—the need to reduce costs—and asked for their advice instead of proposing my own solution.

Your supplier understands their own products and services better than you do. They know where the fat margins are, who the nimble competitors are, and where you are getting the best (and worst) value in your business with them. Ask them for the answers: "I really need to reduce my costs in this area. Can you help me with ways to reduce our bill?"

Engage your supplier as a partner in solving the problem. Letting them propose a solution allows them to be creative and to offer ideas you may never have thought of. It also allows them to find ways to address their own goals while meeting yours. A supplier might be willing to meet your need for lower prices in exchange for your meeting their need for a long-term contract or a more regular payment plan.

The supplier is more sensitive to competition in their industry than you are. This means that even if you have done the research, their response to your request for a lower bill may be better than you expect.

In cases where the supplier comes back with less of a discount than you are looking for, you can bring out your research and ask them for help in understanding it. In some cases when I have done this, the suppliers have explained to my satisfaction why their higher price is worth it; in others, to my surprise, they have acknowledged that I might be better off with a competitor and even recommended one specifically.

I have seen suppliers reduce our costs in a number of ways.

- **Readjustment to market price.** Our CD-ROM producer was realizing continued reductions in their own costs as well as increased competition. We were ordering more units each month at the same price we had been quoted a year before for a smaller volume. One phone call resulted in a 10% price reduction with no discussion.
- **Consistent workload.** A services vendor explained that our unpredictable schedule cost them a lot in resource allocation. If we changed our schedule from 5,000 units this month, 20,000

the next, etc., to a predictable 12,000 units every month, they could reduce our costs by 40%.

- **Reduced services.** When we asked the company that cleans our office space to help us reduce costs, they pointed out that many of the things they were doing every day (like emptying desk-side trash bins) could be done less frequently.
- **Volume discounts.** A supplier who sold us 10,000 units a year in randomly sized orders offered a 25% discount if we simply ordered in 5,000 unit blocks.
- **Alternate products.** Suppliers have introduced us to lower cost alternatives that we were not aware of.

Understand the risks. If you have not taken a close look at your expenses recently, you will find the first round of cost cutting surprisingly easy. If you make this type of belt tightening a regular event in your business year—which you should!—you will find that it gets more difficult each time. You will also risk squeezing suppliers too hard and too often.

Remember that your supplier needs to make a profit to stay in business too. While there are some commodities for which there is so much competition and downward price pressure that you can repeatedly win new discounts (like long-distance phone service), in most cases you will encounter limits and will need to back off and give the supplier time to breathe. It is one thing to be a savvy customer and another to be an unprofitable one. Be thrifty but not miserly.

Specific risks include the following.

- **Being fired as a customer.** We had a successful business relationship with a graphic designer on a fixed-price basis. When we needed to cut expenses, we agreed to scale back both the fees and the work. Within three months, the designer dropped us as a client, so he could focus on fewer, larger accounts.

- **Hidden increases.** If you squeeze too hard with a supplier that sends variable bills, you may see your savings billed back to you in other ways. If you push down an hourly rate by 10%, for example, you may find projects taking 10% longer than they did previously.

- **Loss of goodwill.** Certain suppliers are critical to your business. You want your relationship with these key suppliers to be profitable and friendly so that if you have a critical need or an emergency, they are willing to step in and help you.

No one will fault you for wanting to trim your expenses. In most cases they will even help you. They will fault you, however, if you don't recognize their need to make a profit too. Approach cost cutting with suppliers in a considerate and collaborative way, and don't burn any bridges you may need to cross back over in the future.

Adding 5% to Your Income

The 5% you are looking for to make a difference in your business is not sales; it is profit. While there are lots of ways to raise profits by cutting expenses, there is only one way to increase your profit margin from the income side: raise prices.

If your business is forever hovering on the edge of profitability, your pricing may be at fault. Small businesses in particular tend to underprice their products and services as well as to underestimate their true cost of sales.

Worse, many businesses are setting prices based on their costs instead of the value they are offering the customer.*

---

*See Jeffrey Fox's *How to Become a Marketing Superstar* (New York: Hyperion, 2003) for more on this.

Unless price is your competitive advantage and number one business emphasis, you should raise your prices right now.

Five percent would be easy, but the few customers who do obsess about price may leave you, and the rest won't care about the difference between 5% and 8%, so make it 8% to be safe.

I'll wait here while you do that.

Now that you have raised your prices, you should review everything you offer to customers to ensure you are making a profit on all of it. Classic blind spots include these.

- **Shipping charges.** Don't just pass through your shipping charges; add on a handling charge. Your cost to ship something is far in excess of what the shipping company charges you. Unless you have built shipping into your standard pricing, in which case you should not charge for it at all, you should be adding on your handling costs and a profit margin.
- **Payment plans.** If you are offering your customers the option of paying over time, you should be charging them for that convenient service. Be sure to include the actual cost to you, in deferred access to the cash and in the administrative overhead, as well as a profit margin.

While nickel-and-diming customers with add-on fees and special charges can be very annoying, selective use of these fees can be a way to increase your margin without adjusting your core price. Banks, airlines, car rental companies, and cellular service providers have abused these fees, adding as much as 30% to base prices, but that does not invalidate the technique or its effectiveness.

Add-on fees can be particularly useful when you are in a business where advertised prices are very competitive and where there's enormous variability in cost by location or time of year.

Finally, you need to offer something with enormous margins to that small but valuable group of customers for whom price is no object. There are people out there who always want the best. There are people who place a huge value on convenience. If you can offer a premium extra that doubles your profit on a sale, you only need a small number of customers to take that extra to significantly increase your overall profit.

> Most customers won't notice or care about the extra fees, but some do. Allowing customers to opt out of some fees in exchange for opting out of the associated benefits can soften the impact of the fees. For example, many car rental companies charge a Frequent Flyer Surcharge of up to two dollars but allow customers to opt out of it in exchange for forgoing the miles normally earned by a rental.

You can offer premium extras as add-on products or services or as alternate versions of your standard offerings. Create options that double (or triple) your margin and that are clearly optional purchases or upgrades. You do not want to antagonize your core customer base with out-of-place pricing. You want to offer something extra special that does not appear necessary to your price-sensitive customer but which is attractive to your price-insensitive customer.

Start with a concept and imagine how it would apply to your offerings.

- **Private reserve.** Offer a premium version of your food product: handcrafted, specially chosen, or extra-aged; packaged in a distinctive way.
- **Super-Rush processing.** Beyond rush, there is the option of going to the front of the line for immediate processing or same-day delivery.

- **Personalized.** Offer personalization or customization of products for which it is not normally available.
- **Special edition.** Create your product with different materials. Offer bonus content or gift packaging.
- **Personal training.** Offer in-home installation and training or a special direct line for support.

I ran my university's weekly newspaper for a year. The paper was printed in black and white except on the front page where another ink color was used for the banner. The way the paper was printed and folded, the same color plate ran against the back and two center pages but was rarely used on them. There was no incremental cost to use the color on those extra pages; there was just a limited amount of space there. We charged 50% more for color ads and began to ask every advertiser if they would like to add color. When 5–10% of the advertisers did, we were able to increase the overall profit in each edition by 2–4%.

To price your premium offering, take your per-unit margin from a list-price sale. Add on the incremental cost of the premium quality product, service, or packaging you are considering. Don't be afraid of premium prices 50–100% over your list price.

Conclusion

When times are tight, you can always find 5%. Often you will find 10–15% or more. As nice as that is, it usually means that you have waited too long to look.

Reviewing your expenses and increasing your margins should be an ongoing process. Do the full review at least twice a year, and engage your employees and suppliers in the whole process—looking at both the income and expenses.

Calculate 5% of the annual revenue of your business. Would adding that amount to your bottom line make a difference? Start looking—you can find it.

10 Profit Is Why You Are in Business

Everybody understands that businesses exist to make a profit. Profit is so much a part of how we understand our society that when an organization is set up for any other purpose, we explicitly label it a "nonprofit" organization.

Maybe because it sounds greedy, small businesses in particular do not generally talk about profit. Instead they focus on their secondary purposes: to help individuals find the best life insurance at the lowest rates; to provide a worry-free roofing future; to bring the authentic taste of Chicago deep-dish pizza to Podunk, Wisconsin.

Unfortunately, many people get so wrapped up in the secondary purposes of their business that they lose sight of the primary purpose. I was one of them.

Profit Enables You to Pursue Your Other Goals

In the early days of my business, I was consumed with growth and with "the mission." We sell Bible software, so it was not difficult for me to see our work as something nobler than just making a profit. I believed that success meant providing our useful tool for Bible study to as many people in as many countries in as many languages as possible.

Business is about numbers, and I was a true devotee of the numbers. I tracked gross revenue, employee headcount, number of customers, countries served, and languages supported. I made decisions based on growing those numbers. A lower price will sell more units? Let's lower the price. A single customer asked for a Swedish version? Let's build a Swedish version.

It wasn't that I completely ignored profit. I checked in once in a while to see that we still had one. I just didn't worry too much about how big it was, and I did not take the time to find out exactly where it came from. In a high-growth business like ours, I reasoned, we were investing in the future, not trying to make money right now.

Rapid growth, some outside investment, and some very profitable projects held trouble at bay for a few years. But when it caught up with us, it hit us hard: on sales of $4.6 million, we managed to lose around $900,000. It had been our best year by every other measure. We had higher revenue, sold more units, and employed more people than ever before. We had simply failed to make a profit. In the months that followed, our continued losses threatened our survival. I began to realize that if we did not make profit the focus of our efforts, I would have neither the luxury of pursuing our mission nor the convenience of a place to live.

Around the time we reached this low point in our business, I attended a meeting of entrepreneurs. Introductions revealed that the man sitting next to me had a locally focused service business a fourth the size of mine. He did not have a quarter-million customers in 140 countries in a dozen languages, and he did not have ambitions to change the world. He did, however, have a consistent profit of 10%. His goals lacked the global scope of mine, but he was actually accomplishing his and making a positive impact locally. For all our size and ambition, the impact I was then most likely to make was an increase in local unemployment.

Making a profit is what enables a business to accomplish its mission. Profit needs to be the first priority, or you will not have a chance to pursue any others.

There Are Lots of Ways to Be Unprofitable

Our huge losses forced us to take a careful look at our business. We discovered that under my careful direction the company had successfully navigated into every major profitability trap:

- **We fell in love with our customers.** Our customers are some of the nicest people in the world. We sell to pastors, students, and missionaries—people who have chosen giving over earning and who do not have large budgets. We wanted them all to have our software, so we kept putting out lower and lower cost configurations until every potential customer could afford it. We wanted them to love us too, so we spent huge amounts of time doing lots of little things individual customers requested even if they were only of interest to that one customer.
- **We valued quantity over quality.** We believed that the number of people using our software was the most important metric. We did not distinguish good customers from bad customers, and we would sell at any price to increase the customer count. We put products into cheap "box-o'-stuff" collections and offered ridiculous discounts for site licenses and other high-quantity sales.
- **We created work to keep the staff busy.** When we found ourselves overstaffed (easy to do when you value increasing headcount), we invented new projects just to keep people busy. Without any concern for the size of market, we once developed a cuneiform word processor (really!) just to keep

some programmers busy for a quarter. Over three years it had a grand total of $350.40 in sales.*

- **We took projects at a loss to keep a competitor from getting them.** We told ourselves that we wouldn't lose money; we would just have a very small margin. The reality is that we wanted to win the contract so badly that we were willing to deceive ourselves as to our real costs. "It's strategic," we told ourselves.

> The use of the word *strategic* should set off your alarms. In business it rarely refers to strategy anymore; it has become a code word that means "losing lots of money."[1]

- **We failed to correctly account for costs.** When we were bidding projects or planning new products, we used only unburdened costs in our calculations. We accounted for the raw cost of goods and the actual wages associated with the labor, but we made no allowance for the overhead that goes with all the costs: raw goods were handled and stored; people sat on chairs at desks on floor space we leased. Our team was supported by receptionists and bookkeepers and other personnel whose costs we failed to associate with any specific project.
- **We lost a little on each unit and tried to make it up in volume.** By promoting the extra value to the consumer, we were succeeding at getting more customers to choose our top-end product instead of a less-expensive configuration. We were excited to see this happening but confused as to

*This product actually enjoyed a monopoly on the cuneiform word processing market and was successful in terms of winning a large share of its potential users. But even 100% of that market would not have made it a profitable project; all the people in the world writing cuneiform script could meet in my kitchen.

why we were not making even more money. When we were finally forced to sit down and do a real cost analysis, we found out that this product had more than twice the raw costs we thought and that we were losing money every time we sold it. And we were up-selling more and more users to this money-losing configuration every day.

At the heart of all these bad decisions was a fear of losing business or missing opportunities. What I failed to understand back then was that losing unprofitable business is a very good thing. Why would anyone want unprofitable business? Something that is not profitable is not an opportunity; it is a waste of time.

Everything You Do Should Be Profitable

Impending doom is a wonderful motivator. I had signed personal guarantees; if the business failed, I would go down with it. Facing, at last, the prospect of personal ruin, I became obsessed with profitability. As an organization we attacked costs, promoted sales, and developed a powerful new decision-making system to help turn our business around:

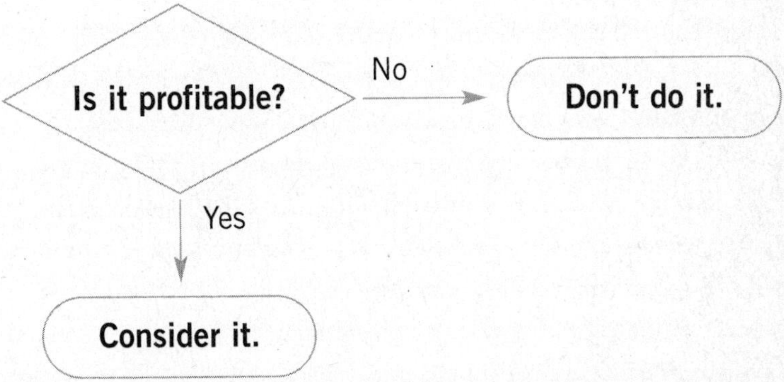

As you can see, the new system did not add too much complexity to our decision-making process. It was relatively simple to implement. It did, however, make a big difference in our business.

In one of the first applications of the new decision-making system, we evaluated the business prospects of a new piece of software we had developed. We were confident that there was a large market for it but realized that it was outside our core audience. We did not have access to the right customers or the resources to establish ourselves in this new area.

We sold the software to another company that was already established in the new market. The deal was profitable for us and allowed us to stay focused on our primary product line. I was very proud of our newfound responsibility in finding a profitable alternative to an unprofitable foray into a new market.

A few weeks after the deal closed, the buyer asked for some extra work from our programmer. Feeling good about the fact that we had made a profit on the deal, I prepared an estimate based on our cost for the programmer's time. "It's still profitable," I told myself.

Then my internal alarm sounded. The software sale was a done deal. Contracting out the programmer's time was a new deal, and I was planning to do it at cost. In fact, it would not be at cost; it would be at a loss, since I was not accounting for overhead or lost time on our own projects.

I doubled the quote for the programmer's time to ensure I covered all our overhead expenses. Then I doubled it again to make sure it was profitable. And then I rounded it up to a nice, even sum.

I was sure that the buyer, who knew the value of a programmer's time, would balk at the inflated quote. But the buyer happily agreed because he was wiser than I was. The buyer expected me to make a profit when selling him services just as he expected me to make a profit when I sold him the software. He, in turn, expected to make a profit on the programmer's work when he took the product to market. Why else would either of us be in business if not to make a profit?

Stand Firm for Profit

Few customers have the temerity to ask you to take their business at a loss. Most will at least give lip service to your need to make a profit. They would just like to define your profit as a positive number approximating zero.

Like an endless stream of new car buyers waving "actual dealer invoices," your customers will constantly attack your profit margin. They don't wish you ill; they just need a little discount, and surely, in your big, fat profit margin, you have room to move just a little bit, right?

Don't do it! Stand firm! You do not really want to join the car dealers in a world where every sale is a battle and customers worry that they got a worse deal than their neighbor, do you?

If your price is too high or your margin too fat, you will find out soon enough: you won't have any customers at all. If that is not the case and your price and profit are right, then you do not need to bend for any single customer. Making an exception to avoid losing one deal or one customer is like making one hole in a dam. It won't be long before your leak is a flood.

Put Profit First

Profit is the first mission of every business. It protects and enables all the others. Goals may inspire your business, and cash may keep it alive, but if your business is not pursuing a profit, it is not a business; it is a hobby. Or a money pit. Or a massive black hole that will absorb your time, effort, hopes, dreams, and financial future. Take your pick.

When we learned the importance of profit in my business, we not only changed our decision-making process, we changed our spreadsheets. We hardwired a minimum profit margin into every financial decision. Our budgets have a fixed-percentage profit allocated before any other costs; profit is the only unassailable line item.

We regularly produced products on a contract basis for a much larger company. This company had rigid internal systems to ensure profitability. Their employees were virtual slaves to the spreadsheets; if a project did not hit the numbers, it did not happen.

As the small contractor, we had gotten into the habit of accommodating our customer. After all we were small and agile, and it was big and inflexible. We quoted each project based on our costs and profit margin. Costs were difficult to estimate perfectly but reflected our best guesses and actual experience. If it turned out that the project did not work on their spreadsheets, the customer's product manager would come to us, and we would squeeze our own numbers. Since we knew that the cost estimates were imperfect, we would reduce those estimates. We would be optimistic about the labor required and would even sacrifice some of our profit margin. We would do whatever it took to hit our customer's target numbers.

As I prepared to sign off on yet another adjustment—we had quoted around $42,500 for a project the customer had only budgeted $40,000 for—I pulled out a calculator. We were giving more than a 6% discount on the whole project. That didn't sound too bad, except when I realized that we were simply planning to do the same work for less money. The $2,500 was all coming out of profit where it represented a huge percentage if not the whole profit (depending on the actual final costs).

I said no and expected to lose the deal. Instead the customer simply struck $2,500 worth of work from the project scope and turned it into something that was profitable for both of us.

The spreadsheets that constrained decision making at our large customer's offices were not any better at precisely predicting sales than our spreadsheets were at precisely predicting labor costs. They could have nudged sales projections up as easily as we could have nudged cost projections down. But they had the discipline to respect their numbers in order to protect their profitability. That made it all the easier for them to respect us, working together to find another solution, when we began to show the same discipline.

In my personal finances over the years, poor planning or unexpected expenses have caused me at one time or another to be late paying a bill. I have never missed an income tax payment, though, because it is withdrawn from my paycheck before I receive it. Having the taxes set aside before the paycheck is drafted ensures their priority.

While we were learning the discipline of putting profit first, we used this same technique. We physically set aside our minimum profit margin from each day's sales out of that day's cash receipts. By immediately taking the profit out of our working cash, we protected it against erosion from unexpected expenses. We were forced to track sales and costs more closely and to be more careful in our planning because the funds allocated to profit were taken out of the equation. In the course of each year, our overall profit still varied but rarely below that set-aside minimum.

Profit can be defined as what is left of your revenue after you have covered your expenses. That is a risky definition for something that protects your business future and enables you to accomplish your business purposes. Define profit as the priority, not the leftovers. After all, profit is why you are in business.

11 If You Are Not Growing, You Are Shrinking

There are only two kinds of businesses: growing businesses and shrinking businesses.

The people running growing businesses know that they are growing. They are seeing new customers. They are seeing new faces around the office. They are seeing higher balances in their bank accounts.

Tragically, the people running shrinking businesses often don't realize they are shrinking. They think they are seeing a temporary downturn. They think they are seeing a seasonal variation. Or, most dangerously of all, they think they are seeing a stable business.

There are no stable businesses.

A business is like a hot-air balloon: it is going up or it is going down. It is never standing still. The change in altitude may be slow, even imperceptible, but if the air in the balloon is not being heated up, then it is cooling down. Cooling down is the natural tendency—you have to actively do something to keep heating up the air. If you do, the passengers are headed for the sky. If you don't, they are headed for the dirt.

Burning at Both Ends

The natural tendency for businesses that aren't actively growing is to shrink. It is easy to believe that a business isn't shrinking because it is maintaining its top line revenue, but the shrinkage that kills many businesses is not on the top line; it is on the bottom line. Your bottom line shrinks, and eventually disappears, when expenses creep up from below and prices fall from above.

This is easy to understand when it happens in big steps, but it's just as (or even more) dangerous when it creeps up on you a few percentage points at a time.

Inflation Is a Nasty Monster

Every year, inflation raises your costs by at least 2–3% whether you are paying attention or not. Being the greedy, attention-loving monster that it is, inflation finds some important commodity or service (oil or health care, for example) that it can spike every year by 20 or 30%—an increase you are sure to notice.

It doesn't take long for an annual 2% increase in all your costs to eat away your profit margin. But it would be a luxury to only have to fight macroeconomic inflation. The steady march of inflation is nothing compared to the big cost increases your employees can demand from your payroll.

One popular measure of inflation is the consumer price index. The CPI is a tasty basket of eggs, bread, milk, and unleaded gasoline that your employees are buying every week. That basket is getting pricier all the time. Your employees are feeling this inflation in their wallets and expecting you to make it up every other week in an envelope. And this is only the first of their reasonable demands.

Employee Value Can Grow Faster Than the Economy

The bigger cost increase comes from the fact that individual employees, unlike loaves of bread, are not commodities. Many of your employees are becoming more expensive because they are increasing in value at a rate greater than that of inflation. Your employees are learning new skills, building relationships with your customers, getting training, mastering systems, and acquiring institutional memory. Time is turning your salesclerks into account managers and your junior project managers into senior project managers. As people learn, grow, and take on more responsibility, they become more valuable as employees. They want to see that increased value reflected in raises and bonuses.

Now some businesses can, for the purposes of payroll math, treat employees as commodities:

- If you have a business where your entire staff turns over at the end of each college semester, then you can perpetually employ the same entry-level worker.

  You may employ Tom, Dick, and Harry this year, but they are all just John Doe college students at entry-level wage.
- If you have a huge company, then you can keep moving people up and through the organization without changing the overall number of bodies in the well-defined and consistently compensated career slots A, B, and C.

  Tom may be hired for Job A, Dick promoted from Job A to Job B, and Harry from Job B to Job C. But Jane is retiring from Job C, so everyone got promoted and you still have the same payroll.

In these cases you may be able to restrict overall payroll growth to the national averages.

Most businesses, though, don't have an endless supply of open rungs on the career ladder into which they can advance employees. But they do have a significant number of employees each year whose personal growth and value as employees is outpacing the already expensive inflationary pay increases. Your Tom in Job A may be ready for Job B, and equivalent pay, before you have a Job B.

Paying for that value—turning Job A into Job B—means increasing your overall labor costs significantly. Refusing to pay for that value means turning over those positions, hiring a new junior clerk to replace that former junior clerk who inconsiderately grew into a competent, experienced senior representative you could no longer afford.

Price Pressure Is Building

Wal-Mart and other retailers are squeezing product manufacturers for lower prices every year. Warehouse stores are lowering prices by selling more and more items in high volume. Competition from China, India, and the rest of the world is creating pressure for lower prices in a wide variety of goods and services. Manufacturers of plastic toys and consumer electronics are no longer the only ones worried about off-shore competition: emerging economies are providing professional and medical services remotely and manufacturing every type of product.

In this environment, it can seem like an achievement simply to maintain your pricing from year to year. But maintaining your pricing means shrinking your business: if your costs are increasing 2% or

Stuck At the Price Wall

For years my company has priced products for a nickel below a nice round number: $99.95, $149.95, $299.95, etc. A colleague at another company once chastised me for this, explaining that, in his opinion, prices like $97, $153, and $302 would have been much wiser. Among other reasons, these whole but not-quite-round numbers can be more easily adjusted as costs change.

The $299.95 product hasn't had a change in price for years because we have been reluctant to break the $300 wall and our well-established pricing pattern. Going from $299.95 to $305.95 seems awkward. But accumulating years of 2% inflation have effectively reduced our revenue for this product by as much as 10%. A $302 price would have been easier to move to $307, $311, etc., over time.

more each year but your prices aren't increasing by the same amount, then your bottom line is being squeezed in the middle.

Your employees and vendors will explain to you how inflation (both the macroeconomic and the personal-value kind) is a powerful force that needs to be addressed by an increase in your costs. Your customers don't want to hear about higher costs from you, though. Last year's price list will be just fine unless you can trim it down a bit, which would suit them even better.

> Sushi restaurants serve a variety of dishes with high variable costs. The market price for different kinds of fish can change dramatically in a short period. Some restaurants have expensively printed color menus with set prices. Others let you choose items from a conveyor belt or floating boats; the color or style of the different plates corresponds to a price on a card. This system removes friction from the pricing process: when costs change, it is easy to adjust the price for a specific plate style or to move a specific item from one plate style to another.

I recently visited a used bookstore where, as in most used bookstores, the prices were written in pencil on the first page of the book. I found a book I wanted for $40, which I felt was a reasonable price for that title. But after comparing it to the other two copies on the shelf, I discovered that the next one was $30, and the last one $22. I bought the $22 copy, which was identical in every respect to the $40 copy.

In the time this store had been in business, the value of this title had almost doubled. It was almost impossible, though, to track that change in value and revise all the prices when the information was stored only in pencil marks.

The largest used bookstore I have ever visited has abandoned the pencil marks for computer-generated slips of paper with pricing information. By logging the prices in a database, they are able to ensure that newly acquired books are priced the same as the copies they already have. They can revise prices as demanded by inflation or changes in the value of specific titles. They can track when prices were last adjusted and even know when to lower prices in order to turn over more stock. And no pencil-equipped customer can revise a price before coming to the counter.

Like the used bookstore that computerized, you need to look for ways to make your pricing flexible. You may not be able to raise your prices every year; you may be facing pressure from customers or competitors to reduce your prices. But if you have flexibility in your market space, then you should make sure you aren't being held back by your own systems or policies: design your business processes to allow you to raise prices when you can.

Growth Is the Answer

The only way to stop your business from shrinking is to grow your business. Growth is about more than just financial measures, though they are important. There are lots of ways to grow that have positive side effects in addition to preventing your business from shrinking.

- **Growth in gross revenue is a lot of fun.** It is everyone's first measure of business growth and the one that, if you grow it quickly, can land you plaques, press coverage, and placement on a lot of cool lists. (Placement on these "fastest-growing companies" lists will in turn land you a lot of cold calls from office furniture salespeople.)
- **Growth in employee headcount lets you do more.** The more employees you have the more you can get done, and the more brains you have solving problems and coming up with new ideas. Sure, employees can bring you headaches:

scheduling, personal problems, interoffice rivalries, etc. That comes with the territory. But, for all the hassle, people are always the most productive assets.

- **Growth in product line can be a way to plan for a bigger future.** Diversifying your offerings provides insulation against a downturn or setback in one category and helps drive growth in all the other parts of your business.
- **Growth in space is inspirational.** There is just something about using an entire building or occupying a whole city block that feels good. Stepping into empty, newly acquired expansion space makes you feel light on your feet. Nothing says "the sky is the limit" like a warehouse in which you can't see the ceiling.
- **Growth in customer base is safety.** Customers are what feed the whole business. Adding more customers means increasing revenues or, at the very least, becoming less dependent on a small number of customers.
- **Growth in locations is aggressive.** When you open the second store or office, it is like staking a claim for doubling your business. "Whatever we did here, we can do it all over again there."
- **Growth in vision is leadership.** When your vision expands from seeing what you are doing today to seeing everything you could be doing tomorrow, you are positioning yourself as the leader in your business and in your industry.

Many people want to grow their business in every way. Others look at some, or all, of these growth measures as more trouble than they are worth. Maybe you don't want to manage more people. Maybe you don't want to open another location. Maybe you are happy with the money you are making and don't want to take on more hassles.

It's true that growth is a pain. Rapid growth is an even bigger pain, and on top of that, it's dangerous: When you are moving slowly, you can still drive off the road. When you are moving quickly, you can drive off the road and shoot out into space over the ravine.

It may be that rapid growth is not the thing for you. Some growth still should be, though; otherwise, you will wake up one day to find that the slow, steady shrinking of your business has turned it into a straitjacket—or a corpse.

The most important measures of growth are profit and cash: profit because it is the reason you are in business and because inflation is devaluing it every year, and cash because it is what keeps your business in business.

You can grow profit and cash by raising the numbers in top line categories: revenue, customers, products, locations, etc. You can also grow them from the inside by improving processes and efficiency and knocking down costs. Growth doesn't have to be in the obvious outward measures; you can experience healthy growth by changing your inside measures.

> Grow profit and grow cash. Any other growth should be to serve the growth in profit and cash.

Even if you run a one-person business and don't want any new employees or customers, you can still grow by reducing costs, working more efficiently, or even by cutting back your hours while maintaining your revenue.

Money Is Not a Growth Aid

I used to think that the secret to growing my business was money. It made sense: I had lots of ideas on how to grow the business that I couldn't act on because I didn't have enough money. I met lots of people with shrinking (or already failed) businesses who explained to me that the problem was that they were undercapitalized. "If only we'd been able to raise more money," everyone said.

I did manage to raise some money at a time when I thought I needed it. Our growth had slowed, and I thought money would fix the problem. I took the money and, thinking it was a miracle growth substance, spread it all over and around my business.

I was wrong. Money is not a growth aid. Money is an accelerant. There is an important difference.

Money doesn't help a business grow. Money helps a business move faster. The money doesn't care which direction the business is going, and it doesn't do anything to change the direction. If the business is growing, money will help it grow faster. If the business is shrinking, money will help it shrink faster.

When I added money to my business, it was at a time when we had stopped growing and started shrinking—I just didn't know it. I was watching the wrong growth metrics, tracking headcount and product line rather than profit and cash.

Spreading money around my business sped everything up. The overspending went into overdrive; the slide in profits became a headlong fall into losses. Instead of saving the business, more money almost killed it.

Gasoline is another accelerant. In the right circumstances, more gasoline means more power and more speed. In the wrong circumstances, more gasoline means more fire, and the building is burned down faster.

Think of money as gasoline.

Don't Blame the Rent

At a busy tube station in London, England, I saw a retail store with a sign in the window: "Closing Sale! After ninety-five years at this location, we are going out of business."

I was curious about what could close down a retail business that had survived so long. It was in an amazing, high-traffic location. It had made the transition between the founder and more than one successor. It was a reseller of a product still in demand. What fatal blow could end the business life of such a long-standing operation?

It was the rent.

The proprietor blamed the increasing cost of business, specifically the rent. He said that when the landlord needed funds, the tenants got squeezed. At last he couldn't afford to stay in business.

It is never really the rent.

The rent will always go up, like taxes and all the other expenses. The London retailer's rent had marched upward for nearly a century. The growth of the business had met that challenge and many others. The business didn't die because of a final rent increase. The business died because it had stopped growing and had let the rent and other expenses turn it into a shrinking business.

The only direction you want to go is up. Grow cautiously if you must, but do grow. Because there is only one end for a shrinking business: no business.

12 Good Systems Protect You from the Perfect Employee

For a software company, our internal computer systems were a mess. Our databases, Web site, and order-processing system had all been cobbled together by whoever needed them first, with help from whatever employee happened to know something—anything—about the technologies involved.

Money was tight, so we put off hiring someone to manage the systems until the very last moment. When we could simply not understand or manage the systems anymore, we hired Sam and tossed him, like Brer Rabbit, into the thicket.

Sam figured out the tangled systems and began to improve them. For years, Sam did a great job as a one-man department. He knew where everything was and could quickly string together solutions for the endless stream of problems we sent him.

Sam told me if he had more resources, he could organize and clean up our systems. If I gave him some time, he could document the systems, and with some help, he could automate the manual processes.

Things were working, though, and I didn't want to spend more money. "Let's just do the minimum that works and get on to the next project. We have lots to do," I told him.

Sam built an experimental Web site that let us take preorders for a product that we might or might not produce. There were multiple steps on the road from preorders to production, which users could follow on the Web site. Since we were in a hurry to try it out, and because we were not sure that the preorder program was going to succeed, we just had Sam whip up the most basic of systems. To our customers it looked like a slick, automated process. On the back-end Sam had to manually step orders through the different stages of the process.

The project was a huge success, and so we began to offer more products through the preorder system. Sam wanted to improve the system, but I needed him on other projects; besides, since the manual steps were a week or more apart and only took a few minutes, it didn't seem worth the investment to build a system. Sam could just do it.

And it worked. Until one Friday when it was time to run the final and most important step of a preorder process—the placing of the orders and the charging of all the credit cards—and Sam was out of the office.

I tracked Sam down by phone and told him we needed to process the orders. "I can do it when I get back," he said.

"We need to do it today," I said. "Is there anyone else who can do it?"

There was no one else who knew how to do it, but Sam agreed to try to talk Joe through the process. I went on to other things.

Later that day, like the first crack in a dam, an employee mentioned a curious phone call. A customer was wondering why her credit card had been charged five times for the preordered product when she had ordered only one copy. While we were investigating that, another call came with the same question.

Curiosity turned to panic. I went looking for Joe.

It turned out that the system Sam used to process the orders was just what I had asked for: the minimum that would work. It did not have much user interface. It did not have any status indication. It did not have error messages.

When Joe clicked the button to process the orders, there was no indication that anything had happened. So he clicked it again. And again. And again, until he gave up and checked with Sam. Sam explained that one click was enough; everything happened quietly in the background. Each click initiated placing all the orders and charging all the cards, unless interrupted by another click.

Without knowing it, Joe had processed hundreds of preorders five times each. But not all of them; some were processed less than five times, depending on when the process was interrupted.

The accounting team immediately began to sort through the orders and to manually credit the overcharges back to customer credit cards. There were hundreds of orders to manually examine and process, but we hoped to finish before anyone else noticed.

We didn't.

It turned out that lots of people monitor their credit card balance daily. It turned out that lots of people use credit cards that are tied directly to their checking accounts. It turned out that we caused some customers to overdraw accounts and bounce checks.

I had visions of losing our credit card–charging privileges, of lawsuits, and of going out of business.

We managed to clean up our errors quickly. We reversed the charges before they went onto statements, we apologized profusely, and we compensated those customers who were inconvenienced. We dodged the bullet.

Sam was a perfect employee. He did everything asked of him, and he rarely made a mistake. He did things quickly and to the minimum requirement, just as I wanted. He didn't waste any time on documentation.

Joe had made a simple mistake, using an undocumented tool he had never seen before.

I was to blame for the nightmare. I had encouraged, cultivated, and relied upon a perfect employee.

Who Are the Perfect Employees?

The perfect employees are the ones who remember everything and who never miss when shooting from the hip. Perfect employees do not work from a checklist and are not following an operations guide. Perfect employees are self-directed. Perfect employees have it all in their head.

In a small business it is especially easy to grow perfect employees. Often they are the first people you hire who stay with you, or the first people you hire for a specific function. When you have been doing something yourself and finally hire someone else to do it, and she does it well, you plant the seed of a perfect employee. It is often such a relief to turn over responsibility for a job that, when it is done well by a self-directed employee, you begin to count on her to just get it done.

An easy test for perfect employees is to play fill-in-the-blanks:

- "I don't know how we do that; _____ always takes care of it."
- "We would be in big trouble if _____ quit."
- "I don't know what I would do without _____."

If your blanks read "Norman," then Norman is a perfect employee, and you have a problem. Because if your perfect employee steps in front of a bus, you will be lying on the pavement next to him.

The Proverbial Bus

You can never know when an employee is going to step in front of, or on, a bus. One minute you have the perfect employee who is taking care of everything for you, and the next minute he is gone, and you have no idea how the software works, who to call to reorder the raw materials, or where the key to the file cabinet is.

No amount of loyalty, good health, or compensation can save you from the buses.

- **The career bus.** Most perfect employees have the courtesy to give you two weeks' notice before moving on to another job. Some only tell you on their last day.
- **The medical bus.** A heart attack or other medical emergency can snatch away an employee in a moment. Often the employee's return date is far off and unknown, which makes it difficult to hire someone else to take over the job. You are left in medical limbo.
- **The moving bus.** Her mother got sick. His spouse got transferred. Their foreign visas were finally approved. For all of these reasons and more, I have lost key employees, suddenly.
- **The prison bus.** Even the best of employees are not necessarily the best of citizens. An unexpected arrest can rob you of a good employee. The prison bus steals the innocent from the office as well: jury duty is an open-ended commitment over which you have little control.
- **The actual bus.** Cliché though it may be, some people *do* get hit by a bus. Sudden death is always a tragedy for friends and family; it can be one for your business as well.

Even a single employee sick day can disrupt your business if it takes the perfect employee away on the day when you need what only she knows.

Good Systems Are the Solution

All of my business with Martin's company was through his partner Peter. After Peter was killed in a car accident, Martin had to take over Peter's responsibilities, including the relationship with us.

After a lengthy visit to our offices, Martin expressed his admiration for our business. Privately, he shared his concerns about our haphazard organization: "You have a lot of good people, but you don't have any good systems. A good business needs good people *and* good systems. They support each other."

Martin was right. All throughout our business we had perfect employees doing a great job, but each of them was an island. There was poor communication among them and no documentation on how each island worked—or even all the things it did. Losing one of our perfect employees would have set us back significantly, if it did not wipe us out completely.

What Is a Good System?

A system is a process for getting things done. A system can be as simple as "put the heaviest items at the bottom of the grocery bag" or as complicated as a 1,200-step process for making a self-winding wristwatch.

Every business is a combination of people and systems. The problem is that the systems are often inefficient and undocumented, trapped inside the heads of the people who created and execute them.

A good system is a system that is efficient, documented, and continually being improved. Good systems may be exceptionally well executed by one person, but they are designed and documented in such a way that they are not dependent on that person. If the person who runs a system is suddenly unavailable, it should be possible for someone else to take over the system. The documentation for every good system is available to you and to your employees.

Good systems have several advantages.

- **Good systems are not dependent on specific individuals.** A good system may require talent to execute (assembling a watch movement, writing a press release) but may be executed by other talented people. The documentation explains all the steps of the process.

- **Good systems facilitate consistency.** A good system for responding to inquiries, cooking a hamburger, or packing a box ensures that your product and service appear consistent to your customers no matter how often you change who is doing each job.
- **Good systems reduce fraud.** It is more difficult to commit fraud if the systems for placing an order, approving a payable, and cutting a check are transparent, documented, and reviewed by multiple people.
- **Good systems prevent lockouts.** Are there two copies of the key? Does more than one person know the administrative password to your server? Are the account names and passwords for online services recorded?
- **Good systems scale.** A good system can be replicated. The one person executing the system can become two people executing the system. Scalable systems are essential to manageable growth and create efficiencies in the process: you only have to develop and document the system once in order to see the benefit many times over.

Good systems have backup plans. Good systems *are* backup plans.

Obstacles to Good Systems

There are two primary obstacles to developing good systems.

Systems are a hassle to create. Documentation is a pain to write. It is always easier to just do something than to teach someone else how to do it. It takes even more effort to write the documentation on how to do it.

Once you have gone to the trouble of documenting something, it is difficult to keep the documentation up-to-date. The documentation may be printed, and changing it requires finding the source documents and revising, reprinting, and redistributing them. If the documentation is in audio or video format, it can be even more expensive and difficult to revise.

Systems need accountability. Even the best of systems fail when they are not executed correctly. A good system needs accountability to ensure that it is followed correctly.

Many restaurants and retail outlets have an inspection and cleaning checklist on the wall just inside the restroom. This list has to be initialed at regular intervals after the restroom has been inspected and, if necessary, cleaned. This is a perfectly good system to ensure clean restrooms. It is a useless system if there is no enforcement.

I was washing my hands at the sink in a restaurant bathroom when the door opened, and an arm appeared. The arm quickly scribbled initials on the checklist on the door and then disappeared. I never saw the employee whom I presumed was attached to the arm, and the employee never looked into the messy restroom.

It was clear that this restaurant enforced the restroom checklist system to the point of ensuring that every time period on the list was initialed. It was also clear that there was no inspection of the inspection system. The result was a system that accomplished nothing but interrupting employees every hour on the hour and reducing customer confidence in their operations: If this is their process for inspecting and cleaning the part of the restaurant I can see, how bad is their process for safe food handling?

Make It Easy to Build Good Systems

The most important thing you can do to encourage the development and use of good systems is to make them easy to create. Your employees will follow your example in designing and executing good systems, and they are more likely to help create them if it is easy to do.

Make it easy to document a process and design a good system. Even more importantly, make it easy to revise and update the documentation. The more "friction" there is in the process of revising documentation, the less likely it is to happen.

In my company, we started with libraries of word processing documents stored on our file servers. These documents were written with a lot of care and then printed out and made available to whoever needed them. They worked well but slowly went out of date as our processes matured and changed. No one had responsibility for reviewing or updating the documentation. The people actually working the process did not have the ability to revise and redistribute the documentation.

We tried a company intranet, which is an internal Web server with a structured system of documentation. The intranet was encumbered with security controls and was difficult to update. Even after training no one could remember the procedure to update a procedure.

Ultimately, we switched to a wiki. A wiki is a special Web site that can be hosted inside or outside your organization

Shoot It

Some things are easier to show people than to explain in writing. A point-and-shoot digital camera with video support is an easy way to record processes without a lot of hassle. We used a cheap camera to record the process for locking the doors, setting the alarm, and changing the canisters on the soda pop machine in the kitchen. You do not need any special equipment or software. The small-format video clips these cameras record are copied over just like still digital photos, and they are perfect for playback on a computer screen.

and which can be edited by anyone who can see it. It is very simple; it involves no fancy procedures. Every page has an edit button, and after clicking it, anyone can easily revise the text on the page. A record is kept of every change, and anyone can step backward to see earlier versions of the page.

The wiki makes it easy to document a process, and that reduced friction makes it easier to develop good systems and keep them up-to-date. Every system is available to everyone and is easily revised whenever necessary. We store in the wiki everything from how to process an order to the company phone list to the schedule for our chili cook-off. The wiki itself has become a good system: "put it on the wiki" is the system that ensures that company knowledge is recorded in a place everyone can access.

The wiki works for my company because everyone sits at a computer; you may need a different solution. What is important is to find the simplest system that will work for managing your systems. No matter how complicated your processes may be, if documenting and managing them is not simple, then you will never turn them into systems.

How Do You Think They Got So Big?

Small businesses often resist building good systems because systems look a lot like the big company rules and bureaucracy that the small business was created to avoid.

This is, of course, completely true.

Big companies are very system driven. At the start, they may have been as chaotic as any other small company, but in order to get to where they are, they had to develop good systems. As your business grows, your need for systems will grow also.

It is important to find the middle ground between no system and chaos and a world of unnecessary red tape. A large company may actually need an automated, Web-hosted, multistep system for approving

> In order to take two hours to visit the doctor, a friend who worked at a big company had to fill out a paper form, get his manager's approval, and mail the form in advance to a central personnel office a thousand miles away. He quit and started a small company.

and ordering new business cards. That system would be a waste of resources in a small business.

Implement systems that enhance your business, that minimize your risks, and that help your employees do a better job. Be alert so that you do not implement systems that are ridiculous or out of proportion.

The Other Kind of Perfect

Before our customers all had e-mail and the Internet, we used to mail out literature packets in response to telephone inquiries.

Some customers were impatient and would call back within a day or two to say they had not received the literature. There was no way to tell if the literature had not yet been sent, if it had just been sent the day before, or if it was lost in the mail.

To solve this problem, Mary in the mailroom was instructed to keep a mail log. This handwritten record of all outbound mail could be consulted when a customer called to see when and where a package had been sent.

When we decided to do a large mailing to our customer list, we generated a few thousand labels from our database. Mary was given tubs full of these computer-addressed packages in order to apply postage and put them in the mail.

The following day, the packages were still in the mailroom, which seemed reasonable. The day after that, they were still there. And the day after that, there were still hundreds of unmailed packages. It did not seem like it should take so long to apply postage.

It did not take that long to apply postage. It took that long to handwrite the name and address from every computer-generated label in the mail log.

Mary was the other kind of perfect employee. Mary followed systems perfectly and never dared to challenge or change them. Mary was just as dangerous and expensive to the business as the self-directed employee who never used any systems.

Good people and good systems complement each other; neither works alone. You always need to be watching out for the perfect employee.

13 The One Who Writes Wins

My grocery list makes for more interesting reading than the average contract. And the only thing worse than reading a contract is writing one. It seems that for every point you want to address, there are a dozen definitions and subpoints that need to be fleshed-out in detail.

My business is all about contracts. We're constantly acquiring and granting licenses, engaging outside service providers, and developing custom projects for other companies. You could wallpaper a house with the contracts I've signed.

Negotiating all these deals is fun; writing them up is not. In the early days of the business, when we'd get to the end of the negotiation, the person across the table would often ask, "Would you like me to write this up and send it over to you for review?" Relieved, I would say yes and thank them for performing the service. It seemed like a great deal: the other party would do the hard work of writing up the contract, or cover the expense of having an attorney do it, and then I'd get to review it. The deal was already negotiated, and there was plenty of time to review the document before we actually signed.

Stupid, stupid, stupid.

I should never have passed up a chance to write the contract.

Why You Should Write the Contract

In simple terms, a contract is nothing more than the written form of an agreement between two parties. An agreement is reached through discussion and negotiation and is presumed to be something that both parties find acceptable. A contract is written that describes the particulars of the agreement; you sign it and file it and hope to never see it again.

And in my experience, most contracts are never seen again. Most of the people I've done business with are fair and honorable. They self-enforce the terms of our agreement even when it's not advantageous to them, and they are usually flexible when circumstances change. The contract is a dusty, old text that is respected but seldom consulted.

When there is a disagreement in a relationship, however, or a difference of opinion on the interpretation of the agreement, the contract becomes something quite different. The dusty, old text takes on all the characteristics of a sacred manuscript. It's inspected with a magnifying glass; definitions are looked up; phrases are parsed and reparsed to extract new meanings. Worst of all, you may discover that the text plainly commands something you wish it didn't.

The person least likely to be surprised by the detailed reading of a contract is the person who wrote it. That is reason enough to write it. There are other advantages as well.

- **Framing the debate.** The first written description of the agreement serves as the basis for the final contract. The draft contract presents the terms that describe the agreement, defines the meaning of those terms, and effectively creates a set of boundaries within which the final agreement is reached.

  Even if the major deal points are worked out, there are still lots of minor points that need to be addressed. The writer chooses which points to address and writes the full treatment for all of them.
- **Padding the contract.** There are many reasonable, small points you can add to a contract that add obligations or

benefits for each party.* A list of these points that exclusively favors one party will generate resistance; a balanced list is less likely to do so. The writer can choose both the concessions she is willing to make and the advantages she would like to have.

- **Owning the little stuff.** There are lots of little things in a contract that don't seem that important because they're so unlikely to be used. In the glow of mutual agreement and bright hopes, it may not seem that important to worry about which jurisdiction will govern the contract, what arbitration method will be used, or what the process for remedying breaches is. To argue with reasonable choices on these points in the draft contract seems almost rude. That's all the more reason to be the person making those choices.

Most contracts are formidable pieces of text. Size alone grants the drafter an advantage because the other party most likely lacks the will and patience to argue any but the central points. If you write the contract, you will often "win" the minor points by default.

How to Write a Good Contract

The first step in writing a good contract is not calling your attorney. Yet.

A contract is a legal document, but it is a legal document about a business issue. You know more about your business issue than your attorney does. (If this is not true, you should make it true before signing any contracts.) It is easier for you to learn the legal issues related to your business issue than it is for your attorney to learn your business

*In my industry I have learned about lots of small but useful things that can be added to a contract, from employee discounts to marketing funds to special conditions for deferred payments. They are all reasonable, but they are not all obvious. Take every opportunity you can to read contracts in your field to learn what is reasonable and possible.

issue. And it is a lot more valuable too: over time you will benefit more from an understanding of the legal issues in your industry than from paying your attorney to learn your business.

I do not mean to minimize your attorney's expertise. Your attorney probably knows a lot about general business legal issues and is an invaluable help if you are in a dispute. You need to understand general business legal issues yourself, though, and having your attorney tutor you is not the cheapest way to learn.

For standard contracts that deal with general issues like employment, leases, and work-for-hire, you will find software packages, books, and Internet sites with a variety of prewritten contracts in word processing format. These contracts are more like forms that you can either use as is or modify for your purposes.

Good contract templates exist for many specialized needs as well; you will be surprised at how specific a document you can find on the Internet.

If you are in an industry that involves a lot of contracts, you should be able to find a specialized collection of stock contracts that you can purchase or subscribe to. This is a good investment and an excellent resource not only for contracts but for learning what kinds of deals are being done in your industry, since the example contracts are often derived from actual projects.

Reading several different contracts on the same subject is a good way to learn what points yours should address. I have also found it useful to go back and review the contracts that larger companies have written and signed with mine. Those contracts are typically long and extremely thorough. Many of the contract points that end up in a large company's standard contract reflect lessons learned at great cost. You can get the benefits of that expensive education by discerning the reasons behind those points.

For every point in a contract, there is some circumstance under which it could become the most important issue. Some points, however, are more likely than others to become the impetus for wailing and gnashing of teeth.

- **Duration of the contract.** Many contracts are forever. That is great if you are buying real estate but a bad idea for lots of other deals. My company has received and granted licenses that have no end. I regret the ones I have granted and am sure the licensors regret the ones I received.
- **Fixed prices.** Interest rates, commodity prices, and inflation are numbers we know are variable. More dangerous are the numbers we think are fixed or that we wrongly believe we control. Markets change, and product lines are sometimes dramatically repriced. Setting all your numbers to percentages with maximums can protect your costs; percentages with minimums guard your income.
- **Renewal terms.** At signature time, the end of the contract may seem pretty distant. Do not forget to address renewal terms. If you are "getting," you will want the right (but not the obligation) to renew "not unreasonably withheld." If you are "giving," you will want clarity on the conditions under which you can choose not to renew. I learned this lesson the hard way when a long-term license to content that was a key part of my product expired. A change in staff and policy had ended the licensor's interest in my business even though it was profitable. We had to scramble to reconfigure our product when the "routine" renewal was declined.
- **Selling the future.** What distinguishes a new product from one derived from an older product? When are two products part of the same "family"? On exactly what will someone have first right of refusal? Vague definitions in contracts have won and lost fortunes. It is tedious but worth the time

to spell things out clearly. Make sure you know if you are doing a deal for today or one that includes today and tomorrow; make sure the contract reflects your understanding.

Do Not Send an Editable Contract

It is easy to e-mail the word processing files for a draft contract to the other party for review. Don't do it! Send a read-only copy in PDF format or even on paper.

There should be only one editable version of the contract, and it should be in the hands of the person who is drafting it: you. This simple precaution prevents innocent misunderstandings that can arise when the parties are looking at different versions of the contract. It ensures that you, the person drafting the contract, have to review and type any changes to your draft. This helps eliminate unnecessary tweaks or wording changes by the other party: when you have to write a request for every change, you are discouraged from all but substantive changes.

My friend Anne-Marie learned this lesson the hard way after signing a lease agreement. She had given the real estate agent the master document so that the agent could integrate details from both parties. After a long back-and-forth negotiation, she signed the final copy the agent printed and which appeared to reflect the final agreement. It was not until weeks later that she discovered that the agent had made a subtle, last-minute change in terms at the lessee's request, believing it to have been with her knowledge. The change cost her thousands of dollars.

Of course we should all be reading what we are signing, but the reality is that at the signing table, there is rarely the time or the will to go through the whole contract again. It is better to have brought the document you drafted and controlled.

While not appropriate for every contract, a walk-away clause is a powerful tool to ensure balance in the future. If your deal is designed to continue to benefit both parties into the future, you can back that up with a clause that lets either party walk away from the deal on a few months' written notice. This type of early termination gives both sides an incentive to keep the relationship equitable and time to remedy imbalances.

When the final draft of the contract is ready, you should send it to your attorney for review. By waiting till the end of the process, you ensure the best use of your attorney's expensive time. You should also be specific in your instructions. You do not need the attorney to rewrite your contract in legalese. You do need the attorney to point out significant omissions, technical errors, and unenforceable provisions.

The draft contract you send to the other party should always be complete and ready to be signed. Even if you know there will be a few rounds of revisions, you should send a document with both the terms and the boilerplate (addresses, definitions, etc.) ready to go. A finished document conveys your readiness to move ahead and discourages trivial changes.

When You Cannot Write the Contract

I would like to say that I now draft every contract I sign. Unfortunately, I can't because I do not have a monopoly on this great concept. Sometimes the other company wants to draft the contract. If the company is big enough, and if I want the deal more than it does, the other guys get to write the contract. (For example, a first-time author who wants to get published and a big-time publisher with an in-box full of proposals.)

When you are stuck being the other party to someone else's contract, you can

- **ask for the word processing files.** You can always offer to make your changes to the draft directly in the word processing files; you can volunteer to do the final edits and print the signature copies. This gives you a chance to take on at least some of the writing and to know the revision history of the final draft.

- **introduce a third party.** The contract defines a business relationship, and arguing the minutiae of a one-sided contract can strain that relationship right from the start. Even after you have negotiated the major points of the deal, an attorney, accountant, or agent can be introduced to help finalize the contract. It is bad business to renegotiate the key points once they are agreed upon, but with the right instructions your third party can honor the deal while advocating for balance in the minor contract points.

- **walk away.** More than once I have walked away from a supposedly finished deal because of the contract. All the best intentions and mutual goodwill do not change the fact that the contract is the final authority on the business relationship. If you do not like the terms in the written document and are not willing to live with them, then you should just walk away.

Contracts Rule Your Business, So Rule Your Contracts

Now, when I reach the end of negotiations, I am the first to say, "I will write this up and send it to you." We go back to our own library of templates and existing contracts and try to get a first draft out within one business day. We are taking the initiative to own the master document before the other party decides to write it up, and it helps ensure that the written contract reflects a fresh understanding of the negotiations.

Taking control of writing your contracts is not just about winning an advantage over the other party or reducing your legal bill. I want a fair deal no matter who writes it up, and I am willing to invest in legal advice when I need it. It is about developing confidence and expertise with the documents that define your business relationships.

> A good contract is good for both parties. A great contract is one you write.

14 Read

You can learn everything you need to know in order to make your business a success by reading.

The good news is that you are reading right now. And you are reading this book, which indicates that you read about business. And that you are especially intelligent, discerning, and good looking. The bad news is that you are not reading enough. Specifically, you are not reading a wide-enough variety of material in large-enough quantities.

To say for certain that you are not reading enough would be presumptuous except for the fact that it is always true. You cannot read enough. But the more you read, the better it will be for you and your business.

Why Reading Is Good for Your Business

Saying that reading is good for you is a lot like saying that exercise is good for you. Both statements are true and generally accepted. And there are people who naturally ignore and people who naturally act on the wisdom of both statements.

If you are a natural reader, I am suggesting ways to expand the stack of material at your bedside. If you are not a natural reader, I am here to make the business case for your conversion.

Types of Reading

The reading that makes a positive impact on your business falls into a few categories.

- **News.** The latest who, what, when, where, how, and why. News is where you find out that your biggest customer just laid off 20% of their workforce, that the street your shop is on will be closed for construction, and that your product just got a great review. Reading the news (local, national, global, and industry-specific) gives you the facts you need to be forewarned of risks and opportunities.
- **Inspiration.** Whatever your troubles, someone has suffered worse. Whatever your challenge, someone has overcome a larger one. Whatever you think of your own limitations, someone who is far more stupid than you are has accomplished much more. Inspirational reading helps free you from fear and challenges you to do better.
- **Technical knowledge.** How-to information is available on everything from getting a loan to managing a restaurant to filing a patent. Reading for "how-to" not only addresses immediate needs, it prepares you for the future by introducing you to information you do not need yet but will. All too often I find out that the clever solution we came up with in response to a new problem is not a new solution at all. It was just new to us. We spent a lot of time and money reinventing something we could have found through reading.
- **Ideas.** There are no new ideas. What we think of as new ideas are really just new applications of old ideas. And you can learn all of the old ideas from reading. The more uses of the old ideas that you read about the easier it will be for you to apply the ideas to your business.

- **People.** Your business is about people: employing them, working with them, purchasing from and selling to them. You can learn a lot about people by spending time with people. You can learn even more about people by spending time with books. Reading about people in particular, whether real or fictional, helps you understand how and why people act as they do. Reading about people in general helps you improve and expand your business by better understanding—and thus better serving—different groups and cultures.

What to Read

- **The Internet.** What can I say about the Internet that has not already been said? It is the searchable, full-text companion volume to the multimedia experience that is the world.* As a reference tool it is indispensable, though famously inconsistent and unreliable. It is also something you can read to your profit. The Internet serves as more than just an index or repository of words and images; the Internet is the home of the zeitgeist. Particularly in interactive forums, the Internet is where you find out what is hot now.

  Search the Internet for your business, your competitors, your customers, and your vendors. Read the blogs, the newsgroups, the rants and raves and rumors. Count the hits on the search engines and read between the lines of the discussions. Reading the Internet is listening for the buzz.
- **Periodicals.** The Internet may be more up-to-the-minute, but it has no editor to provide quality control. A search engine will return peer-reviewed academic research side by side with

*The Internet has emptied the metaphor barrel.

lunatic conspiracy theories. Periodicals are fresh, edited, and delivered to your mailbox—what could be better?

I used to feel as though I was wasting money if I did not read every issue of everything I subscribed to. I started dropping subscriptions until I wised up to the fact that it is not a crime to just skim the table of contents. Most annual subscriptions are a bargain even if I only get one useful thing out of them each year, and even in the worst cases I usually find something truly valuable at least every other month.

- **Newspapers.** For me the more local the newspaper the more useful it is. The local paper has the latest news on what really impacts my business day-to-day: what is happening in my city, my neighborhood, and even on my street. Many cities also have business journals that focus on local people, businesses, and business-related government issues. These local business publications are great for building your network, staying aware of local regulation and taxation issues, and finding opportunities for hiring, space, and partnerships.
- **Magazines.** A lot can be learned from the stories of other businesspeople, which you can find in national business magazines. General news magazines provide insight into major events and cultural issues that affect your business. Make it a point to read the magazines that your customers subscribe to as well.
- **Trade journals.** It is indeed a rare business that is so unique that there isn't a relevant trade journal. Trade journals are a great place to get ideas that are directly relevant to your business. Even the advertisements are useful.

  Don't limit yourself to the journals for your industry; the boundary lines for industries and categories are always shifting. If you run an espresso stand, the specialty-coffee trade journal may be exactly right for you. You would find value in reading the quick-service restaurant journals too. Trade journals for adjacent categories will prompt you to think outside your normal operations. And your competitors are less likely to be reading them, so you will be getting practical ideas that they are missing.

- **Academic journals.** The best and worst of reading can be found in academic journals. A subscription to an academic journal that touches on your business, product, or service is guaranteed to provide something exciting enough to keep you up all night as well as hundreds of pages of text that can help you get back to sleep.

  I think of academic journals as my secret weapon. Some of the best and most unique features in our product were inspired by things I found in academic journals. In some cases, ours was one of the first commercial uses of an algorithm or idea that had been widely published and discussed in journals for years. So much of the academic world does such a good job of insulating itself from the business world that the commercial value of what the academics develop can remain hidden for years. There are huge rewards for the businesspeople who invest the time in reading the literature, deciphering the academic-speak, and slogging through all the useless by-product of the "publish or perish" mandate.

  A great investment is a day at the nearest university library talking to a librarian and scanning the tables of contents of journals in order to identify the ones that would be useful to you. Books with titles that start *Readings in (area of interest)* are overviews designed to introduce students to the academic literature in a given field. These are excellent starting points for getting familiar with field-specific academic vocabulary and usually contain, or point to, the best papers on the subject.

- **Books.** Books are not the timeliest material you can read, but they are more likely to contain the timeless material. Books are better organized, better edited, and better at holding open a door.

  The obvious starting point for books is your area of business: If you are a florist, you should be reading about flowers. If you run a software company, you should be reading about software. And if you run any business at all, you should be reading about business in general.

  And you are. Good for you.

  When you have finished drinking from this particular fountain of wisdom, you should head back to the shelves and load up. Business books are not the kind of books you carefully select one at a time for patient, deliberate reading. Business books are the kind of books you toss into a cart and purchase by weight.

  Don't get me wrong—many of them are worth reading thoroughly. The problem is that it is hard to know which books are worth that investment up front. If you focus on those books, you will miss all the useful information you can glean from a quick skim of all the other books.

  General business books repeat a lot of the same material. (Surprise: this is not the first book with a chapter titled "Cash Is King.") Specialized business books go into more depth than you may need. For example, I have a book on business diagram types. I got some value and some good communications tips from skimming it quickly. I would not get more value from a detailed reading of its history of each diagram.

  Build a stack of business books, and treat it as a resource, not a task list. You do not have to read it all. You should take the time to skim through the whole stack to identify the books you want to read thoroughly and to extract what useful information you can from as many books as possible.

Reading business books is like panning for gold. You have to handle a lot of gravel before you find a nugget. But the nuggets are worth it.

- **Business history.** Books that follow the history of an industry or technology help develop your understanding of big-picture issues. When you step back from a particular person or company, you get insight into how society and businesses change over time. Even more importantly, you learn about failure. The people who led businesses that failed do not write about their accomplishments; they are rarely the subjects of personal or corporate biographies. Business history is where you get to see both the winners and the losers in the same pages. Understanding their relationships and reading stories of their successes and failures help you understand how your market could shake out in the future.

- **Biography.** The good thing about a great biography is that it tells you everything about the subject's life. That is also the bad thing: Who has the time for all those details? Reading biographies takes time, and there are not a lot of shortcuts. But biographies are worth the time because biographies expose the how, not just the what.

  History will tell you what happened. It will tell you who did what, when they did it, and what the consequences were. It will often tell you why they did it. It rarely tells you how they did it because history books are rarely personal enough.

  Biographies—even biographies of companies, not just people—are full of the little details. And in the little details you learn how things happened. A business history will tell you that John Doe started a business and made a fortune. A biography of John Doe will tell you to whom he talked, what he did, what mistakes he made, and what little steps he took that led to success. Biography is history of the how that you can imitate or avoid on a day-to-day basis.

Reading a wide range of biographies is useful as long as you focus on biographies of doers. You can learn a lot from the details of a lifetime of accomplishment, or even from a lifetime of failure. The detailed *how* of doing is worth the study. The biographies of accidental celebrities—those people made famous by crime, disease, or reality TV—may be entertaining reading, but they are probably not useful in growing your business.

- **Novels.** There is still room for fiction in your business reading. Good novels can offer two valuable things:

1. **Insight into motivation.** Good novels help us understand other people. The novelist can explore a character's motivation and thought process from inside the character's mind. A biographer can only guess, and an autobiography cannot be trusted. Only in fiction can we explore the truth of how people think and why they really do what they do.

2. **Windows on other worlds.** Contemporary mysteries, thrillers, and other fiction can provide detailed introductions to real-world settings ranging from government to industry to foreign cultures. A murder mystery set in a bank might teach you a lot about how banks actually work. A novel set in a foreign country might help you understand how to expand your business there. Look for the back-cover endorsements that say things like "The author shows what life in the [car wash/investment banking/pig farming] business is really like."

- **The Bible.** There is a reason the Bible is the best-selling book of all time: it is the mother lode of wisdom. When a CEO friend of mine told me he had never read the Bible, I gave him a copy with some bookmarks inserted. A month later I ran into him and heard that the Bible was on his bedside table. "I was surprised—it's full of stuff on business," he said.

  Chapter 6 of the book of Proverbs is a great place to start for pithy wisdom you can put to use in your business life right away. Many newer Bibles have a topical or word index in the back where you can look up subjects like money, profit, wealth, and business. There are also a number of books on the Bible and business or money.

Summaries Are Not Cheating

While you would be cheating yourself in an English class if you read the notes on Hamlet instead of the full text, it is not cheating to read business book summaries. Subscribing to a summarization service—over the Internet, as a paper newsletter, or even in audio format—is a great way to keep up on the latest business books. The summaries are useful on their own, helping you get the key message of the book in just a few pages, and they help you decide which books are worth the time investment of reading completely.

Reading Benefits Your Whole Organization

The value of reading in helping make your business a success is multiplied when more people in your business are reading.

For years, I assumed that I was the only person in my business who benefited from reading about business issues. Occasionally, I would share a book on sales techniques with salespeople or bring a relevant anecdote or news item to a meeting. But in general, I thought of reading as personal development and everyone's own responsibility.

Over time I began to see the difference in perspective and useful insight of those employees who were reading a lot versus those who were not. The readers not only did their own jobs better, they were able to see beyond their area to the workings of the whole company and the market we are in.

I put all the business books I had read and found useful on a table in our office. I sent out an e-mail offering twenty-five dollars to any employee who read a book from the table and e-mailed a one-paragraph review to the company before a specific date. The more they read the more cash they earned.

> Outside of a dog, a book is man's best friend. Inside of a dog, it's too dark to read.
> —Groucho Marx

The program was a great success. Computer programmers read about sales techniques, and product branding and technical support agents read about leadership and product development. Many of the reviews contained thoughts on how the book was directly relevant to our business and provoked valuable discussions. We saw benefits in improved cross-department understanding as well as a deeper appreciation for how the business works. Each year we repeat the program with broader participation and more benefit.

15 Don't Fly Blind—Build a Dashboard

As the leader of your business, you have a vision of where you want the business to go. As clear as that vision may be, if you do not keep an eye on your instruments, you are more likely to put a crater on a mountainside than to soar in the clouds.

A business dashboard is a concise report that you check every day. It tells you how you are doing and acts as an early warning system for upcoming problems.

A profit and loss statement is not a dashboard. A monthly report is not a dashboard. These financial statements tell you what happened in the past; a dashboard tells you what is happening now. A dashboard can even tell you what is going to happen next.

What to Put on Your Dashboard

Every business needs a different dashboard. There is no single design that is right for everyone although there are common principles and components.

Your dashboard should give you an up-to-the-minute view of your overall business health, the state of your operations, and any numbers that act as early indicators of trouble.

Business health. The health of a business, in terms of its life and death, is reflected in the financial numbers. Cash, sales, and profitability act as the short-, medium-, and long-range measures.

I ran my business without a dashboard for years. Things were going well, and we were growing as much as 100% per year. All of our reporting looked backward: we always knew how we had done in the past year. The only up-to-date information we had was anecdotal snapshots. We could tell you how many units of Product A were sold today but without any context in terms of how many we had expected to sell or how many we had sold at the same time last year, etc.

When our growth slowed down, we noticed. The slowdown showed up on reports a few months after it began. Unfortunately, that was already too late to avoid big problems.

While we were right in the middle of the slowdown, we did not notice it because we were not paying attention to the numbers on a daily basis. Without a dashboard, we had no context and could make excuses for this bad day in sales, or this month that is always slow, or this seasonal lull that is probably normal.

We not only failed to see trouble coming, we failed to recognize it when it was standing at the door.

- **Cash.** Nothing says healthy like cash on hand. The most important part of my dashboard is the cash section. I track how much cash we have, how much cash we have set aside for known upcoming expenses, and the change in our receivables balance.
- **Sales.** Sales are what ultimately generate the cash, so it is good to track sales too. Charting sales against projections that are informed by historical data helps you anticipate seasonal variations.
- **Profitability.** Track profitability as closely as possible. While it may be difficult to calculate profit on a daily basis, indicators like average sales discount, product sales mix (percentage

of sales from each distinct product), and even raw expenses can inform a rough estimate of profitability.

Operations. Your dashboard should give you insight into the state of your operations. You need information on who is doing what and how well they are doing it. This is where you get information on what is driving the health numbers. Some things you might track here include the following.

- **Sales by channel or salesperson.** Where are you getting your sales? What percentage is retail versus wholesale, and how is that changing? What are sales figures for each department or salesperson in relation to each other and historical data?
- **Production statistics.** How many widgets were made today? Is widgets-per-hour moving up or down? What is the error rate in the shipping department?
- **Service metrics.** What is the call volume in the service department? What is the average telephone hold time? How many callers hang up while waiting to talk to someone? How many customers does each technician help each day?

Early indicators. The information on your dashboard helps you understand what is happening in your business. Early indicators are the metrics that help you understand what is going to happen next. These numbers are the leading edge of peaks and valleys in your operations or financials.

The early indicators are different for every business, and it can take time to identify them. The best indicators are often not the obvious ones. It is obvious that today's sales are a reasonably good indicator of next month's receivables. It is less obvious that a change in the ratio of sales to new customers versus sales to repeat customers could result in an increase in customer-service call volume two weeks from now.

Early indicators can be changes in ratios: variation in units returned over number of units shipped might reveal a quality or support problem. Indicators may even be external data: anything from interest rates to the weather could foretell a bubble or depression for your business.

How to Build a Dashboard

The most important thing about your business dashboard is that it is updated and viewed every day. It does not matter so much what technology you use to implement the dashboard as long as it is convenient enough to work with daily.

Most dashboards are based on spreadsheets. They can be delivered by e-mail or posted on an internal Web server. If your business is not fully computerized, you can build a dashboard template as a paper form.

In my company, the accounting department compiles the primary dashboard every morning and posts it to a server where it is supplemented by a number of automatically generated reports. These extra reports allow me to drill down from the high-level view in the dashboard into more detail when I choose.

If the dashboard is overly complex or takes too long to read, it won't serve its purpose. It needs to be something you can look at quickly every day. The best dashboard reports have all the key numbers in one place with the backup detail out of the way but still available.

- **Use charts instead of gauges.** Don't take the dashboard metaphor too far: you do not need colored gauges and meters on your business dashboard. A fuel-gauge style indicator of profitability, with a needle that goes from the red to the green zone, may look cool, but it wastes a lot of space communicating one piece of information. A chart that shows profitability for the past year overlaid on the previous year's data uses the same space but communicates a lot more.

- **Watch trends instead of snapshots.** Today's numbers only tell you what happened today. Maybe you shipped twice as many units today because the shipping clerk was out sick yesterday. Important data should be shown as a trend over a period of time.

- **Months are bad units.** Every month does not have the same number of business days. Every month does not have the same number of weekends or holidays or snow days. Month-to-month comparisons are only useful for comparing this year to last.

  Some businesses use thirteen accounting periods of four weeks each instead of the twelve calendar months in order to allow for more regular period-to-period accounting. Even if you are not willing or able to change your accounting cycle, you can still design your dashboard around more regular periods. At the very least, you can build your charts around the trailing thirty days of data rather than on a month-to-date basis. This will help insulate you from variation in month size and will avoid the weeklong blind spot that comes from resetting charts at the start of each month.

Conclusion

It takes time to build and maintain a dashboard. It may take a year to identify all the data you should be tracking. There is a daily cost in keeping it up-to-date and reviewing the report.

If things are going well in your business, this investment of time may seem like a bit of a waste. The dashboard for a healthy business is pretty boring. This is when the dashboard is most useful, though, because it is when things are going well that you most need advance notice of trouble.

When a business is already in trouble, a dashboard is less useful. If you are driving on a bumpy road, you probably already have your eyes on the potholes. A dashboard with daily pothole counts will not make you any more attentive to the problem. Invest in your business dashboard now for help in spotting the bad roads before you turn onto them.

16 Visit Everyone in Person

Woody Allen famously said that "80% of life is just showing up." In business, that does not mean just showing up for work; it means showing up on doorsteps.

Business travel can seem like an incredible waste of time and money. If you conduct business on a national level, it is not unusual to be looking at two days of round-trip travel to make it to a one-hour meeting somewhere. With airfare, hotel, and car rental, you are facing hundreds of dollars in expenses just to show up. If your business has international connections, it is worse. When you factor in the time and inconvenience, even local visits can seem like expensive distractions.

Trust me, it is worth the trouble. There is no better long-term investment you can make than showing up in person to visit with everyone connected with your business.

Visit Your Customers

Knowing your customers is an idea that gets a lot more lip service than shoe leather. It is easy to think we are in touch with our customers if we are sending them surveys, taking their calls, and answering their questions. We do not really understand them, though, until we visit them where they live. And until we meet them in person, we are just another anonymous and interchangeable supplier to them.

Large and strategically important customers should see a lot of you, in person and at their location. The most important thing that happens when you show up in person is that you communicate that you value the customer and their business. There are lots of other benefits as well.

- **You personalize the business relationship.** It is easy to say no to a stranger on the phone, and it is easy to move your business from Anonymous Vendor A to Anonymous Vendor B. Personalizing the business relationship helps ensure that customers will engage you in conversation. Even after you have left their office, customers are more likely to talk with someone they have met than someone they have not met.
- **You make yourself available for feedback.** When a customer has a problem dealing with a business, it can often seem easier to move on to another supplier than to find the right person to listen to and deal with the issue. In other cases, customers have small but important concerns that they might not take the trouble to call or write about but will share in person with someone who takes the time to ask.
- **You have the time to get to yes.** Sales is about overcoming objections, but that can be difficult to do on the phone and impossible to do by mail. When you are there in person, you can take the time to listen and respond to your customer's concerns and get to yes.
- **You learn how the customer makes decisions.** Are you talking to the decision maker? Does your contact need (or want) to get approval from colleagues in order to act on your proposal? When you visit in person, you can get insight into how your customer makes decisions. You learn about their organization, see how your contacts relate to their colleagues, and often find out how things really get done.

If you sell a consumer product or serve a large audience of small customers, it may be impractical to visit them all. It is still worthwhile to visit as many customers as you can. There may be fewer benefits in terms of relationship building, but there are great benefits in meeting representative customers in person and seeing when, how, and where they use your product.

- **You get context.** Your product is not used in a vacuum, but all too often those of us who develop a product will design it as if it is the only thing a customer will be using at one time. Seeing where and when your customer uses your product informs your design, production, and even marketing of it.
- **You get ideas.** Customers are usually very good at letting you know what to fix in your existing product. They are much less help in figuring out what other products you should be offering them. When you visit in person, you can learn about what customers do when they are not using your product and what other products they are using. These are the idea-seeds for new products and services you can offer.
- **You get the truth.** It's not that customers are not willing to tell you what they do and don't do with your product. It's that they don't think of telling you and often don't even realize what they are doing (or doing wrong). I have watched customers who told me they loved my product and found it easy to actually use it. I am embarrassed to admit that they were often using it in awkward and slow ways because the easy features that I thought were obvious and accessible were not.

Visit Your Suppliers—and Have Them Visit You

What I want to know about my suppliers is that when I place an order, it will be delivered on time, on spec, and on budget. When that is the case, things are fine. But if I do not take the time to visit with my suppliers in person, I may be missing out on opportunities and setting myself up for a disaster.

You want to have a personal relationship with your supplier for all the same reasons you want one with your customers, only from the other

An organization in Europe licenses key intellectual property to most of the companies in my industry, which consists of mostly U.S.-based companies. For years the European organization was represented by a single person who managed contracts and relationships by fax, e-mail, and annual visits to an industry trade show.

All of my competitors had basically the same relationship with the licensor, through this one friendly contact, but I knew that there would be opportunities for a closer partnership in the future as the organization launched a major new project. My company was the leading candidate for that partnership, but the decision was not finalized.

We invested in a trip to Europe to visit the licensor's offices. On the evening we arrived, our longtime contact took us to dinner and dropped a bombshell: that morning he had given two weeks' notice of his departure from the organization.

The next day, we visited the offices. Our contact introduced us to the colleague who would be taking over his responsibilities. We met with the entire upper management of the organization. We toured the facilities, learned more about their business, and ate lunch in their cafeteria. Despite all the business they had done with us and our competitors, we were the first company to actually visit.

A month later our new friend and contact arrived at the annual trade show in the United States. We were the only people he knew; all of our competitors were simply notes in a file folder to him. It was not hard to finalize our selection as the licensor's new partner.

Take the Full Tour

On almost every visit to a supplier, I have learned about a new product or service they offer that interested me. In most cases, it simply had not occurred to the supplier that my company would be interested in this other offering. I had to hear about it during an office tour or see it on a warehouse shelf and ask about it.

Whenever someone asks if I would like a tour of the office, I say yes; I always want to see the warehouse too. Hearing a description of all the office functions helps me understand how the organization works. Seeing the warehouse helps me understand their product line, capacity, and responsiveness.

side. You want to have someone to give feedback to. You want your supplier to understand your needs. You want your supplier to offer new products and solutions to serve your business.

Taking the time to build a personal relationship with a supplier helps keep your interests in mind. If there is a shortage of inventory or an imminent capacity crunch, you're more likely to hear it from a supplier with whom you have a personal relationship. You may even be able to see it in advance during your own visit to the supplier's business. Is their business booming or crawling? Is the warehouse full or empty?

Insist on having your suppliers visit you too. They will be able to serve you better if they understand your business better. I have even had suppliers bring us new business; because the supplier had visited, they understood our business well enough (and with enough confidence) to introduce us to some of their other customers.

Visit Your Competitors

You should never pass up a chance to visit your competition.

If your competitor has a retail outlet, then you are probably already making regular trips to their store. (If not, get going!) If they have an office or warehouse, you should be looking for opportunities to visit there too.

I am not suggesting corporate espionage or breaking and entering. You should not be visiting your competition at 2:00 a.m. with a lock pick and a flashlight. I am not encouraging you to practice reading things upside down across desks.

I am suggesting that you take advantage of whatever public access you have to your competitor's operations (visit the store, drive by the warehouse) and find ways to be invited in for a tour. From your competitor, you can learn information that is not a trade secret or even particularly confidential and put it to valuable use in your business. At the very least, you can learn to put things into proper perspective.

I have found lots of benefits from meeting with competitors.

- **Understanding the real size of the competitor.** When a new competitor entered my market with an impressive array of marketing materials and a very aggressive business strategy, I started to worry. I put more time than I should have into addressing their announced plans until I had the chance to visit with the founder during a trip to his area. He freely shared their company size (two employees) and the fact that they had not yet begun to work full-time, putting an end to my worries.
- **Learning the direction of their business.** Very few businesses are in perfectly aligned competition. There may be a lot more to your competitor's business than the part of it you are competing against every day. By visiting and talking with your competitor, you can often learn where the real focus of their business is or is going to be.

- **Buying or selling assets.** Competitors have similar customers and product lines. This makes them good candidates for buying assets you want to sell or vice versa. I have sold a product line to a competitor for whom it was a better fit and bought one from another competitor.
- **Developing partnerships and joint ventures.** There are opportunities that you cannot afford or do not have the skills to pursue alone. When you take the time to get to know your competition, you can identify opportunities you can pursue together or places where you can share development costs.
- **Feeling the rhythm.** Businesses have a pulse, and you can measure it by simply walking through the facility. A tour of your competitor's office or warehouse can give you a feel for how their business is doing and inform your understanding of how yours is doing as well as the state of your market as a whole.

How to Get an Invitation

My friend Brock received a call from a competitor who was looking to sell his business. The call brought up a lot of questions for Brock: Was he ready to acquire another business? Did he have the resources to do the deal? Was the other company a good fit for his?

My advice? Get on a plane tonight. The opportunity to visit the competition and get the answers to those questions in person, with the

Don't Talk Pricing

It is illegal for competitors to fix prices, agree to serve different market segments, or engage in other anticompetitive practices. Brush up on the law, and ask your attorney about what conversational land mines to avoid before sitting down with the competition.

competitor pitching him on the deal, was invaluable. Maybe it's not a good deal. Maybe now isn't the time for an acquisition. But it is always a good time to learn more about the competition. What he learns during those discussions will be useful whether he buys the company or not.

Use any opportunity to talk with a competitor as an opportunity to visit. Explore a merger or acquisition. Discuss a joint venture. Call and suggest dropping in just because you are in town.

And what if your competitor calls you and wants to stop by your office? Agree to meet—but only at the local coffee shop.

Visit Your Neighbors

It is worth the effort to get to know your business neighbors. Invite them to tour your facilities, and ask for a tour of theirs. Keep an eye out for chamber of commerce–sponsored open houses.

While your neighbors may have businesses completely different from yours, you can still learn something from visiting them. They are hiring from the same labor pool, working with the same local government, and employing the same professional services. Visiting them in person helps you build a personal relationship, share local experience, and understand what resources are available in your community. (When I unexpectedly needed a forklift one day, I knew which nearby business to call; they drove it down the street and helped us out.)

Who Needs to Make the Visit?

In a small organization there is no substitute for sending the boss. When your company is small, you need to be the one visiting on its behalf.

As your company grows, you will need to send out salespeople and project managers to visit your customers and suppliers. While it is important that your team builds personal relationships, you want to ensure that those relationships are with your organization and not just with specific employees. The unexpected departure of a key salesperson can be the end of a customer relationship if the customer does not have any other connection to your business.

We try to have more than one person in the organization involved in our key business relationships; we do not want an employee's departure or unavailability due to sickness or vacation to get in the way of the relationship. Having at least one secondary contact who has also invested in visiting ensures continuity in the relationship.

I cannot make every visit and cannot maintain all the relationships my business has. I do try to meet as many customers and suppliers as possible and to tag along on sales calls and site visits whenever I can. It keeps me connected, allows me to observe my team at work, and communicates to the other company the value we put on our relationship with them. Having the chief executive visit a customer or supplier is a powerful way of demonstrating corporate commitment.

Do You Really Have to Visit Everyone?

My dentist has a sign on his wall that explains why you do not have to floss all of your teeth. It is the same with business:

> You do not have to visit all of your business relationships.
> Just the ones you want to keep.

17 Press Is Yours If You Ask—and If You Want It

My grandfather was a successful entrepreneur. As a teenager, I had breakfast with him most Saturday mornings, getting lessons in life and business over corned-beef hash and eggs.

My grandfather was very proud of my own entrepreneurial efforts and the software company I had started while in high school. One morning, he announced that my story should be in the paper. I completely agreed but had no idea how to make that happen. He explained that it was easy: he would drop a note to the paper and let them know what a great story his grandson was.

I was sure that every grandfather in the tri-state region felt the same way about his grandson and that nothing would happen. But my grandfather wrote a note explaining why my business story was unique and interesting and sent it to the paper. Within a week a reporter was sitting in our den interviewing me for a classic "boy wonder entrepreneur" story. The resulting newspaper clipping helped distinguish my college application; my internship supervisor told me it influenced his hiring me.

Press Can Be Good for Your Business

Press can be good for more than just an ego boost. Press serves as free advertising, which is a valuable thing: any story about your business that is not explicitly negative acts as an advertisement.

Coverage in the news or editorial section gets more attention and has more weight with readers than anything you could put in a paid advertisement.

It is not just your products and services that you want covered. Stories about you and the business itself act as advertisements too. They encourage name recognition and goodwill and can be useful tools for recruiting employees. Some of our best hires have been people who weren't reading the want ads or even looking for a job. They saw favorable news stories on our company's growth or new location and thought it sounded like a great place to work.

Press Can Be Bad for Your Business

It is not true that there is no such thing as bad press. Even basic press coverage can be bad for your business. The deal you make—trading information for exposure—could end up being too costly. You can't control how the press coverage comes across or where it goes. Make sure the trade is worth it.

I love to read news stories about my competitors. My competitors tell reporters things they would never tell me: number of employees, annual revenue, strategic direction, names of key customers, upcoming product plans, etc. Having them get a little press attention is a small price to pay for getting so much valuable information.

> If you compete nationally with a business located in another region, go online or to the library and search their local newspapers.

Many companies will disclose all of this valuable information to a small local paper in exchange for some small local exposure. No one reads the favorable story outside the home market, but the data remains permanently available to all of their national competitors through library and online archive searches. Today, all news is global news. Your message may not reach the whole world, but your facts will.

You Can't Control the Tone

Even if you are careful to share only what you want to disclose, there is no way to control how your story comes out. While a favorable or even neutral story is valuable advertising, a negative story can be an instant death sentence. There's no way to know which way a story is going to lean in the final edit.

Even the most objective presentation of facts can be spun in many ways, and a reporter may have a different and completely legitimate interpretation of your story. One person's economy-building trade with a foreign tribe is another's exploitation of the less sophisticated. One person's strong leadership is another's unreasonable intransigence.

I've seen lots of brutal business stories in which a reporter made a compelling case for the subject's villainy or idiocy in words wrapped right around a smiling pose by the unwitting victim. Those interviewees were smiling at the thought of free advertising; they didn't see the hit that was coming.

What the Press Wants

What the press wants is to be read. And interesting stories are what people want to read. The press is not there to tell your story unless your story happens to be interesting. If you approach the press with a boring story, the press may find its own way to make it interesting. You don't want that to happen.

> Bad press is punishment for being uninteresting.

The first part of having your story told in the press is making sure your story actually is interesting. This is often a problem for businesses seeking attention in the press because the things that make for a good business—consistency, reliability, steady growth, etc.—don't make particularly interesting stories:

LATEST BATCH OF COOKIES JUST LIKE THE FIRST

"We've been running this cookie production line for seven months," said Jane Doe, owner of We-B-Cookies. "And this latest batch of Choco-Delite cookies is just as tasty as the first batch we prepared way back in May. If everyone shows up and the power doesn't go out, tomorrow's cookies will taste exactly the same."

Who cares? Your cookie company is far more likely to get some press with a story like this:

LOCAL GIRL BITES OFF MORE THAN SHE CAN CHEW

The Choco-Delite from We-B-Cookies was six-year-old Mary Beth Jones's favorite cookie—until she bit into one Tuesday and got a chewy mouthful of plastic hair-band.

"It was gross!" said Mary Beth. "I almost threw up."

"Grossly negligent is more like it," echoed local attorney John Smith, who has been retained by the Jones family. "We intend to seek damages from We-B-Cookies and see to it that the Choco-Delite never threatens another child's life."

That is much more interesting, but not the kind of press you want.

Good stories have a hook: something that catches the reader's attention and lures them in. If you identify the hook in your story, you can save a reporter a lot of work. Like you, reporters are busy people who appreciate when work arrives already half done. And you can use the hook to present your story to them, allowing your press release or phone call to stand out from the story pitches they get all day long.

There are lots of classic story hooks that work for businesses. Find the one that fits your business story the best.

- **Rags to riches.** Born into poverty, you worked hard, overcame adversity, and built the world's largest wig factory.
- **Doing the impossible.** They said you couldn't sell dinnerware made from cow patties, but you did it.
- **Small-town boy/girl makes it in the big city.** Your Backwoods Badger ice-cream flavor is picked up for national distribution.
- **Exotic connection.** An ecotour of the rain forest inspires you to import organic nuts hand-harvested by tribal villagers for use in your Choco-Delite cookies.
- **Current events.** Your business builds the newest scanners now required for airport security screening.
- **David and Goliath.** With a fleet of hot-air balloons, you intend to challenge FedEx in overnight delivery.
- **Celebrity.** The star of today's hottest sitcom wore your custom socks on a late-night talk show.
- **Social good.** You developed solar-powered video games for children in places with no electricity.
- **New technology.** You wash windows remotely with a tower-mounted laser that burns away grime.
- **Scandal.** You opened a hair salon where all the stylists wear bikinis while cutting hair in your conservative community.*

If you cannot find a story hook that works, then you probably do not have an interesting story. Waiting is your best bet, though you can always create a scandal if you're in a hurry for some attention.

How to Get a Reporter's Attention

Once you have your story hook, you can write a press release or start making phone calls.

---

*This is the only hook I didn't make up.

Invest the time to identify the right press outlets and even the right editors and reporters to pitch directly. A publication or reporter that specializes in your industry or has covered similar stories in the past is a good candidate.

Be persistent without being annoying. It is a delicate balance but an important one. You want to be available and in mind when the reporter has a hole to fill, but you do not want to be the pestering fool they are looking to punish.

It can be hard to get attention from national or regional media if you have a small business. The good news is that the news business is a food chain. The bigger media watch the smaller media for story ideas, so placement in even a local publication can lead—with a good story hook—to coverage at the national level. My company was once covered in a small local newspaper and then contacted in rapid succession by the regional, big-city paper, a national newsmagazine, and then a national television news network. The story had a great hook

I attended a program for entrepreneurs at Stanford University. Several days into it, someone brought the latest issue of *Fortune* into the classroom. It featured a two-page story on our classmate Brian and his company, 1-800-GOT-JUNK? Everyone wanted to know how he got such great coverage, and Brian explained that it came from calling and asking. That sounded pretty easy, until he told us that it took a *lot* of calling. He called reporters until he found one who was interested. Then he called that reporter more than a dozen times over a period of eighteen months. By the time the reporter had time for the story, Brian had used all of the feedback from his earlier calls to refine his story hook into something really interesting. It was worth the effort. The story in *Fortune* led directly to a story in *USA Today* and from there to a daytime television appearance.

and was able to work its way from the bottom to the top of the media food chain in just a few weeks.

You Are Always on the Record

When you learn to handle a gun, you are taught the first rule of gun safety: every gun is *always* loaded. Along the same lines, the first rule of talking to the press is that there is no such thing as "off the record."

Now, there are times when a gun is technically not loaded, and there are times when a reporter really won't quote you. But with both guns and reporters you only have to forget the current status once to shoot yourself in the foot. Assume things are dangerous, and you will keep your toes.

A Reporter Is Never Your Friend

A reporter may be friendly, but a reporter is never your friend. It's not that they are your enemy; it's that their job is to tell a big, interesting story with consideration from multiple angles. Chances are that they won't agree with you on the most interesting part of your

I recently read a glowing profile of a successful teenage entrepreneur in a national business magazine. The reporter shared the teenager's admission that he sometimes took sick days from high school so that he could work on his business and then quoted him pleading, "Don't mention that to my mother."[1]

How could the reporter resist? The anecdote was perfect for a profile of a teenage entrepreneur and captured the unique challenges of balancing school and work at such a young age. It also exposed the teen's truancy to his parents, teachers, customers, and another million strangers. Worth it, I'm sure—but probably not what he expected.

story, and they may find most interesting the parts of the story you would prefer weren't told at all.

Expect Some Errors

I know my business inside and out because I work with it every day. Reporters who have interviewed me or covered my business have generally had an hour or less in which to learn about something completely new to them. It is understandable that they make factual errors or misunderstand some aspect of the business. The errors are usually on minor points, but they are a consistent feature in all but a few of the stories written about my business.*

I have come to accept this as the price of press, and I don't take it personally. Do what you can to keep things clear. Focus on the theme of the story, and don't overwhelm the reporter with extra information. Always spell out your name.

Provide Help

Create a quick facts sheet or Web page to help reporters get facts, figures, and spelling right. This single page should include the company name and contact information, a paragraph description of the company and major products, full product names and trademarks, full personal names and titles, and all the numbers you are willing to share.

Provide a Web page with publication-ready photographs of you, your facility, and your products. Even when a story is not planned to run with art, a last-minute hole in the layout can create an opportunity for a ready-made illustration.

---

*The most troublesome one was when a reporter covering our relocation to a new town confused my partner and me halfway through the story. Just weeks into my marriage, I was described as missing my un-relocated girlfriend. That clipping didn't go into the family scrapbook.

Respect the Press

An elephant is a powerful animal that can carry a heavy load. It can also sit wherever and on whatever it chooses. Respect the press like you would an elephant.

Don't seek press attention just for attention's sake. Pitch your story to the press when you have a good story hook and when there is a specific benefit to you from a good story. The more thoughtfully you approach your press relations the more benefit (and less risk) you'll realize.

Experience has taught me the bad news about the press: the press is sometimes sloppy, always hurried, and loyal to no one. You never know when it is going to turn on you.

My grandfather taught me the good news about the press: most reporters don't have time to dig up new story ideas, but they have great power to promote you and your business. If you have a good story with a hook that fits their needs, reporters will be glad to hear from you.

18 In Acquisitions, the Buyer Is the Loser

If you enjoy the business of business, you'll *love* mergers and acquisitions.

Sure, the daily challenge of building products, meeting payroll, and providing great customer service has its ups and downs. But that is nothing like the roller-coaster ride of *deal making*.

I love the negotiations, arguing the high value and even greater potential of my business to the buyer. I love the due diligence, being free to probe the dusty corners of the seller's business. I love anticipating rapid growth, of moving ahead by leaps and bounds instead of slow, patient steps.

Making deals is what business is all about. I will sell you my time, widget, or wisdom in exchange for your cash or credit. Deal making for mergers and acquisitions is just a purer form of the business deal. It is not about the products or the services or the people or even the money. It is about the business itself. While people pretend that those other things are the motivation behind a merger or acquisition—and maybe at some early point they are—in the end it is all about the deal. And it's fun!

I have bought four companies and have gone as far as signing a letter of intent to sell mine. I have watched friends acquire and sell businesses of all sizes. And I can tell you that it is always an adventure. And it is almost always the buyer, not the seller, who emerges the loser afterward.

Businesses Are Always Too Expensive

Most business transactions involve an exchange where both parties are getting a good deal. The product or service is worth more to the customer than the cost of it, and the business can provide the product or service for less money than the price it's being sold for. Everybody wins.

There are two things that make this work. The first is the transparency of the transaction. Before making a purchase, the buyer can get enough information (or warranties and guarantees) to know that what they are purchasing will be worth the price, and the seller is getting cash, which has its own inherent value.

The second thing is that most transactions create value. Shovels may be cheap to manufacture in quantity, but 10,000 of them aren't of much use to one party. Sold to 10,000 individuals, none of whom could make a single shovel for the price they are paying, the shovels have value far in excess of the manufacturer's cost.

The sale of a business is different from the sale of a product or service. Generally speaking, the sale of a business is not transparent, and it does not create value. These are the two reasons why businesses are too expensive:

Businesses are abysses. Businesses are bottomless pits of darkness that cannot be fully illuminated. No one understands everything about a business. The only people who come close to fully understanding a business are the people trying to sell it, and they have no reason to explore all its dark crevasses with you even if they could.

Sometimes a business buyer gets lucky and finds a hidden gem deep inside a business. However, the buyer more often finds fool's gold and time bombs.

- **Decaying assets.** Inventory, equipment, furnishings. There are well-established standards for valuing physical assets. None of these standards account for the fact that all of them may be completely worthless to the buyer. How much of the inventory will never sell? Would you buy it today for that value? Would you buy the equipment and furnishings for their listed value? Could you give them away, or will you have to pay to have it all hauled to the dump?

- **Intellectual property and brands.** These are impossible to value correctly, so, to be safe, they are always overvalued by the seller.
- **Integration issues.** Every business has a different culture, different systems, and even a different rhythm. People and processes aren't interchangeable; enormous value is lost just in merging organizations. Key employees may leave, and expensive systems may end up abandoned.
- **Legal liability.** Where the really scary monsters live! If the business has ever had a customer, contract, or employee, there's a lawsuit waiting to happen. You can never know which ex-employee has a grievance or which contract wasn't lived up to or which customer was shipped a faulty product that will soon explode. It could be years before these liabilities are revealed.

Like a movie plot where a character goes to great lengths to assume someone else's identity, only to discover that the person whose identity they have assumed is wanted by the police or Mafia, some companies actually acquire their way into trouble. Alibris, an online bookseller, had a corporate predecessor named Interloc. According to filings for Alibris's initial public offering, "Three weeks after the completion of our merger with Interloc in 1998, we learned that Interloc was the subject of an investigation . . . We pled guilty to criminal charges and paid a fine of $0.25 million."[1] Alibris later withdrew their offering.

No buyer can see a business clearly enough to understand if it is worth the price. It is nearly impossible to value the assets correctly, and it is impossible to quantify the liabilities. And unlike a consumer, a business purchaser doesn't get a thirty-day money-back guarantee.

Businesses sell for their true value or more. A business is a machine for making money. Regardless of what goes out the factory door, the business itself only creates money.

Moneymaking machines never sell for less than the value of the money they are creating (calculated over a given time period). That is the *minimum* price for a business. That means the natural value creation of a business transaction—the difference between a shovel's value to the manufacturer and the consumer—is missing. A purchase transaction causes the difference in the shovel's value to be realized. But a business isn't a shovel; it is just money. There is no difference in the value of money to a buyer and to a seller, so purchasing a business doesn't automatically create value the way purchasing a product does. In the absence of that value, the seller makes the business sale a good deal by selling for more than it is worth.

> Businesses are too expensive because the price includes the best possible value for the assets and makes no allowance for unforeseeable liabilities.

There may be several things about his business that the seller does not know, but the seller does know how much money it makes. And the seller generally knows this in a way that is much more intuitive and subtle than financial statements reveal. The seller knows what is and is not counted a business expense, where the business is frivolous and where it is cheap. The seller wants a good deal, and a good deal is one where the seller gets more than the business is worth to him.

> Businesses are too expensive because there is no value in the transaction itself. The seller can only increase value from the sale if the buyer pays too much.

Identify and Value the Pieces

There are other businesses that have things you could use: recurring revenue, equipment, patents, brands, inventory, customers, employees, etc. These things could be worth acquiring, but only if the price is right and only if you are acquiring assets and not liabilities.

When you are evaluating a business that is, or could be, for sale, take the time to identify what it has that would and would not be useful to your business. For everything that would be useful to you, figure out what you would have to pay to acquire it from the target business. Then think about whether or not you could acquire that asset (or equivalent value) by putting the same resources into another option.

During the crazy days of the dot-com businesses, it was common to see hi-tech acquisitions described in terms of "price per engineer." Three to four million dollars per engineer was considered a normal valuation although deals at $18–20 million per engineer weren't unheard of.[2] Setting aside the fact that these deals were often paid for in inflated stock instead of cash and that the whole world had generally gone insane, there is still something wrong with this picture.

Does it really take $4 million to hire an engineer? Even a great engineer in a hot job market? Wouldn't a $1 million hiring bonus (even in inflated stock) bring in a few recruits? For another half-million you could offer new engineers a full-time masseuse for the duration of their employment, just to relieve the stress of changing jobs.

Unfortunately, the days of poor analysis aren't over. Companies are still overpaying for assets they could acquire for less through other means. I have done it myself more than once; usually because I was lazy. I accepted someone else's number for the value of assets and didn't invest the time and energy to find out what it would cost to develop or acquire the same assets another way. It seemed easier to "buy the whole package" than to build it piece by piece. But the premium I paid was always far more than it would have cost even to hire someone to put it all together.

When evaluating opportunities, I now take the following steps.

1. **Identify the assets.** What does the target business have that my business can use?
2. **Value each asset.** How much is each asset worth to my business?
3. **Shop around for equivalent assets.** Can I find or create an equivalent asset for the same or less cost?
4. **Ask crazy questions.**
   - If I am considering buying customers or employees, what would happen if I took the acquisition cost and offered it directly to the customers or employees in cash instead of paying it to the business they are associated with?
   - Could I acquire these assets without buying them?
   - Could I acquire the value of the customers by letting the other company resell my product?
   - Could I acquire the value of the employees by codeveloping a new product with the other company?

Purchase Just the Assets You Want

If an opportunity passes the value tests, you need to decide how you want to structure the deal. It is possible to acquire all the assets of a business without acquiring the business itself, leaving behind potential liabilities. (This type of deal is something you want good legal advice on, though, because if not done correctly, you can unintentionally end up with the liabilities after all.)

A better arrangement is one in which you only purchase the assets you want. By purchasing a carefully enumerated list of assets (specific product lines, trademarks, facilities, etc.), you may be able to reduce the cost of the deal. You also make it easier to understand what you are getting and exactly what you are paying for each asset.

One way to make sure that you are paying the right amount for each asset is to tie its price to the value you actually realize from it. For example, if one of the assets you are acquiring is a product line, then you might make payments over time based on the ongoing performance of the acquired product line. If you are acquiring a customer base, you could pay a variable price based on customer upgrades or retention following the acquisition.

Variable pricing "earn-outs" for acquired assets may cost more in the long run but can limit your exposure as well as stretch payments over a longer time period. Because they offer the seller a bigger upside if things go well, they can make price negotiation easier and increase the probability that the deal will be fair for both parties.

Reasons to Purchase the Business Itself

For all the difficulties of purchasing a business at a good price and all the dangers of acquiring unforeseeable liabilities, sometimes there are still two very good reasons to buy the whole business.

- **Nontransferable assets.** A business may have a favorable license, lease, or contract that can't be purchased or separately acquired. (Make sure that it is not encumbered by a change-of-control clause that causes it to terminate if the business is sold.)
- **Removing a competitor.** Sometimes there is value in simply taking a competitor out of the market. You might be able to acquire equivalent assets another way, but if you acquire them by buying a competitor, you increase your market share as part of the deal.

Be a Winner, Not a Loser

There are smart acquisitions and unique opportunities. A seller may be retiring or divorcing and anxious to sell. You may be able to acquire an exclusive contract or an unbeatable location. These deals, however, are few and far between.

Examine acquisition opportunities with a critical eye. Don't reject them out of hand; invest the time required to consider them carefully and weigh the costs and benefits. I believe that if you do, you will most often come to the conclusion that the deal is a losing one for the buyer, but you will get a lot of value from going through the process. You will be forced to think hard about your business, to critically evaluate another business, and to investigate new opportunities. Even if you don't do the deal, the process will ensure that you come out a winner.

19 Buy Lunch

You don't have to run a sandwich shop to put lunch at the center of your business. It is already right there, smack in the middle of your workday.

My partner and I came up with the idea to start our business at an all-you-can-eat pizza buffet. Had we not been resting up for a second pass at the buffet I don't know if the conversation would have had the time to wander into the productive area that it did. It was over many more lunches that we nurtured the idea, built the plan, and solicited advice from other people.

Breakfast is about the individual, waking up and starting the day. Dinner is about family and friends and relaxing. Lunch is all about business.

Eating for Business

Meals are a universal experience we associate with pleasant things: conversation, relaxation, and food. It is good business to do business among such surroundings.

- **Meals are more relaxing than meetings.** A meeting is an event where you follow an agenda or topic through to conclusion and then part ways. A meeting may be productive, or it may be a waste of time. A meeting is rarely relaxing.

A meeting set around a meal has a completely different pace. The meal takes time to be ordered, to be served, and to be eaten. The agenda takes second place to the meal. There are lots of opportunities to put the agenda on hold while you think and chew. And, unless your agenda is overly ambitious, there is plenty of time to get to everything.

- **Everybody has to eat.** Meetings feel like time stolen from real work. Meals are time that was going to be spent anyway.
- **A shared meal is a shared experience.** Shared experiences connect people and serve as the foundation of a relationship.
- **Eating levels the field.** As an eighteen-year-old intern at Microsoft, I was scared to death when I ended up on a nine-person team with Bill Gates for a day of team-building exercises during a corporate retreat. What if I choked the world's richest man during the blindfolded rope untangling?

  Sitting on the grass with Bill Gates while he used his teeth to open one of those impossible little bags of corn chips from the box lunch broke the spell. I knew then that I could be a CEO; I opened mine with my fingers.

People Who Manipulate Meals for Power

There are people who use meals for petty power plays. They suggest a quick, light lunch and then order the four-course meal after you choose the soup. Others will encourage you to order an appetizer, soup, and entrée and then ask for a side salad. These are the kind of people who make sure that all the other seats in a conference room are lower than theirs. If you are sharing a meal with someone like this, think of the bright side: it is a quick way to know that this person is not someone you want to do business with.

The Message of the Meal

Every business meal is its own little world. The tone, the goals, and the strategies are different each time. The message of a meal has a lot more to do with the specific participants and the state of their business relationship than it does with a bunch of unwritten rules.

Unwritten rules, of course, are a lot more interesting.

Breakfast. Breakfast meetings are overflow from a fully booked lunch calendar. A breakfast meeting is a favor; it is a concession of personal time to business. If you ask for a breakfast meeting, you are saying, "I know you are very busy, and I wouldn't dare ask for a lunch, but I would really like to meet over a meal."

When you ask for a lunch and are offered a breakfast, the message is, "I am very busy, but I will do you the favor of meeting at breakfast because I am willing to start early for you," or ". . . I am a go-getter who is always at work by breakfast time anyway—aren't you?" or ". . . I am jetting off to Europe in the afternoon."

Breakfast meetings are shorter; it is acceptable to start talking business earlier in the meal.

Coffee. Meeting at a coffee shop is one step up from meeting in an office conference room. (If you don't have an office conference room, then the coffee shop *is* your office conference room.) Coffee is short and implies getting right to business, but in a friendly way.

Going for coffee together, with an employee or with someone already at your office, is different from meeting for coffee; it is more about being friendly than about business.

Lunch. Lunch is the perfect business meal. Lunch is long enough for both the friendly small talk upon which business relationships are built and the time to talk business. It is a meal not generally reserved for family or friends. Everyone has to get back to work, so you know it can't drag on too long; it is easy to escape if necessary.

Dinner. Dinner is the social business meal. It is about hosting visitors from out of town, celebrating the big deal, or getting to know a potential partner or employee or vendor. Dinner is longer than any other meal and can be stretched for hours.

There is plenty of time at dinner; take your time before getting to business. Depending on the purpose of the meal and who is with you, the right time to talk business could be after ordering or not until you have eaten and the table has been cleared. Or even not at all.

Dinner at home. Nothing says you are interested in a friendly, long-term business relationship like an invitation to dinner at your home. Unless you live in a mansion and employ a domestic staff, dinner at your home means dropping your business persona and the trappings of your workplace and letting people see you as you really are.*

Stress-Free Business Entertaining

Having business associates home for dinner can be a lot of work. We have made things easier in my home by developing a standard guest meal. We serve the same simple, low-preparation meal to every first-time guest. It is popular, regional (since we have many out-of-town visitors), contains no food allergens, and it is always perfect since we have made it countless times.

Don't try to impress with the meal; your guests are already impressed by the hospitality. Stick with a simple and stress-free menu, and give your attention to your guests, not your kitchen.

*If you really aren't that nice at home, don't invite anyone over. You can't mask your true self at home.

I have never regretted a business dinner at home. The least I have gotten out of having someone over was a pleasant dinner; in most cases, it has been a big step from business relationship toward friendship.

Etiquette

Invest some time in learning proper table manners. There are numerous books, articles, and Web sites that will guide you through twelve pieces of silverware and keep you from sipping from your neighbor's water glass.

You are going to see them more and more, so take the time to master chopsticks too. But learn on your own time; there is no shame in asking for a fork for as long as you need it. No one cares about the implement you are using as long as you are not flicking food at them with your clumsy stick handling.

Don't worry if you cannot recognize the fish knife or if you have not mastered the finger bowl. You can ask. It does not matter if you prefer the European or American style of holding the silverware. No one cares. In our increasingly casual world, you will be forgiven every shortcoming at the table but one: opening your mouth with food in it.*

Who Do You Buy Lunch For?

You buy lunch for everybody.

Employees. I try to take the people who report to me to lunch or coffee on a regular basis. Getting out of the office one-on-one allows time to get to know people beyond their job responsibilities. People talk more openly about how they feel about their work and work environment when they are away from it.

---

*I know you know that. I know your mother taught you right. Yet it happens all the time. *Do they know I'll never want to sit across a table from them again?* I wonder. *Do they even know they're doing it? Am I doing it and not knowing it?* Ask your spouse. Ask your kids. Make sure you aren't a disgusting dining companion.

The quiet pauses that are part of having a conversation at lunch are what make the time so productive. Lunch is where you get the real story because it is often the only meeting you have with an employee where there is enough time to get below the surface business issues. Lunch is where . . .

- you get the real project status;
- you find out what is going on at home that is impacting work;
- you hear the employee's perceptions of their coworkers;
- you learn what motivates your employee.

Lunch is also a great place to brainstorm. Some of the best ideas we have had in our business have come from leisurely lunches. When you meet in the office, there is pressure to finish the agenda and get back to other things. There is not the same pressure at lunch to stay focused and realistic. You can discuss the ridiculous and fantastic at lunch without worrying about wasting time—it's just lunch. These open and casual conversations are often the seeds of big ideas.

Customers. You have competitors who want to take your customers away. The only thing keeping your customer from becoming your competitor's customer is some combination of what you offer and the customer's own inertia.

- You are offering a product, service, or price that beats your competitor's.
- Your customer does not want to switch providers. It is a hassle to switch; buying from you is comfortable and familiar. They know you, and they may feel some level of loyalty to your business, brand, or to you or one of your employees personally.

It does not matter which factor is the most important part of your customer relationship. Whatever advantage you have with a particular customer is fading under attack from your competition.

It is clear that you need to be talking to your customers. You need to be hearing their concerns and soliciting their ideas. But it is difficult to get this information from a sales or support call. You need to take your customers to lunch. When you do . . .

- you are building a personal relationship that will engender trust, open communication, and, hopefully, a certain amount of loyalty. You may not be able to hold on to an account with personal loyalty alone, but it can make the difference when a customer is on the edge.
- you are learning about your industry and your competitors. Want to hear the word on the street? Want to know what is coming down the road? Give people the time to talk it out.
- you are making it easier for the customer to complain. There are lots of little things that annoy customers but which don't seem worth complaining about. When the supermarket cashier asks, "Did you find everything okay?" it is easier for customers to say yes than to mention their unfulfilled desire for a sesame cilantro-flavored bagel or their frustration that hot dogs and buns aren't both sold in packs of eight.

  Lunch is conducive to sharing the little complaints or the trivial concerns that, left unaddressed, eventually end your relationship with the customer. A friendly meal and conversation create a comfort zone in which a customer can finally say, "It is just a little thing, but . . ."
- you talk about the future. Lunch gives you the time to lay out your vision. You can go beyond your sales pitch and talk

about your plans and how your business will be an even better vendor to your customer in the future.

- you learn about your customer's needs. To plan for the future, you need to understand the customer. It is not enough to listen to what customers say they want. It is not enough to let customers suggest improvements to your product. You need to understand the customer yourself so that you can design or invent the product the customer could not imagine but will not be able to live without. Lunch is where you can put aside the product or service at the heart of today's transaction and learn more about the customer in general.

If your customers are local, build a rotation schedule, and take them to lunch on a regular basis. If your customers are far away, try to arrange your visits to include lunch.

Everyone else. Buying lunch is an easy way to get to know people, build your network, and learn new things. You don't need a great reason to invite someone to lunch; any excuse will do. My line is, "I would like to learn more about what you do. Can I buy you lunch?" It rarely fails.

It doesn't matter if you are not good at small talk. You can still be a popular lunch date if you remember two things.

- Everybody likes to talk about themselves; you only need to prompt them.
- Pick up the check.

Other People to Take to Lunch

- **Local government officials.** Your mayor or city council member. Be more aware of the politics that really affect your business day-to-day: local politics.

Buy Lunch for a Crowd

Some of the most important and influential customers I have are professors. Professors purchase and use our product. More importantly, when they use it, they often recommend it to their students. There are more students than professors, so it is important to us to sell to professors so that they can help us sell to students.

The problem is that professors are busy and difficult to reach. They are scattered around on hundreds of campuses, and you never find them in their offices.

We chose a region with a large number of professors we wanted to meet with and planned an invitation-only presentation around a free lunch at a centrally located airport hotel.

The event was a huge success. Even though we had to limit the number of professors, they came from the whole region and even flew in from other states. We were able to make our presentation to one-hundred key customers at once. The professors got to talk with friends and colleagues they normally saw only at conferences. Our team was able to speak one-on-one with almost everyone.

We have replicated this type of event on a much smaller scale, too, inviting local customers to our office for a free lunch, to meet each other and to talk about our products.

Plan a regional event. Host a meeting of local customers at your office. Buy lunch for a crowd, and give them room to enjoy each other in addition to hearing from you. It is cheaper than advertising, and it is more effective.

- **Other business leaders.** Build your network; learn from their experiences. Spend time with people with dramatically different businesses.
- **Business community professionals.** Raise your profile with someone from the economic development council or the

chamber of commerce and broaden your perspective on the local economy.

- **Nonbusiness contacts.** The principal of your child's school, a pastor or religious leader, or someone from the arts. Your business is part of a larger community from which you draw employees, customers, and connections.

Every Lunch Is an Opportunity

Working right through lunch is a false economy. The value of that extra time at your desk or in saved expenses pales in comparison to the cost of a lost opportunity to learn or grow or to invest in an employee. If you skip lunch or eat lunch alone, you are wasting opportunities.

The world is full of interesting people. Start buying them lunch.

And, if you find yourself near Bellingham, Washington, have your people call my people. We'll do lunch.

20 Winning Takes 51%

There is a lot of inspirational stuff out there about giving 110%. That is great, though possibly exhausting when it comes to effort. But success in business is not about how hard you work. Breaking rocks with a hammer is very hard work that will never put your name on a skyscraper.

Success in business comes from winning more than you lose.

You win by making the right decisions. And the good news is that you do not need to make the right decisions anywhere near 100% of the time. You just need to make the right decisions more often than you make the wrong decisions.

When my partner and I were preparing the very first release of our software, we hired someone to write the documentation. We were busy with finishing the software itself, so instead of investing time in finding the best possible writer, reviewing portfolios, and getting multiple bids, we went with the first person we found and paid him a significant part of our start-up funds.

The resulting documentation was a disappointment, and I felt terrible about our large and largely wasted investment. My father told me to get over it. "If that is the biggest mistake you make," he said, "you will be fine." And he was right. We were fine even though we continued to make mistakes, some of which were much larger. (I later paid another documentation writer four times as much for even less output. I have a blind spot when it comes to documentation writers.)

We were fine because we made good decisions that outweighed all of the bad ones. We chose the right technology, we implemented the right features, and we took the product to the right market at the right time. Thanks to my father's advice, we did not get hung up on having chosen the wrong writer, and we did not waste time and money trying to fix that bad decision. We learned from it and moved on.

Keep Making Decisions

I see a lot of businesspeople who are so concerned with making the perfect decision that they do not make any decision at all. (Okay, I even do it myself sometimes.) They squander time, money, and—most important—opportunity while they collect all the information they could possibly need to make the correct decision.

If you wait to make a decision based on all the facts, then it is about history, not the future. And history is for courts and scholars, not businesses.

Good decisions move businesses ahead. Bad decisions move businesses ahead too. The sooner you make a decision, the sooner you move ahead. (Of course, the type of decision involved and just how good a decision you make are important too. We will get to that in a moment.)

When you make lots of decisions, you increase your forward momentum. Businesses where decision making is slow or fearful get left behind.

For any given decision there is a line that stretches from "no information available" to "all the facts." Your decision is moving from the start to the end of this line.

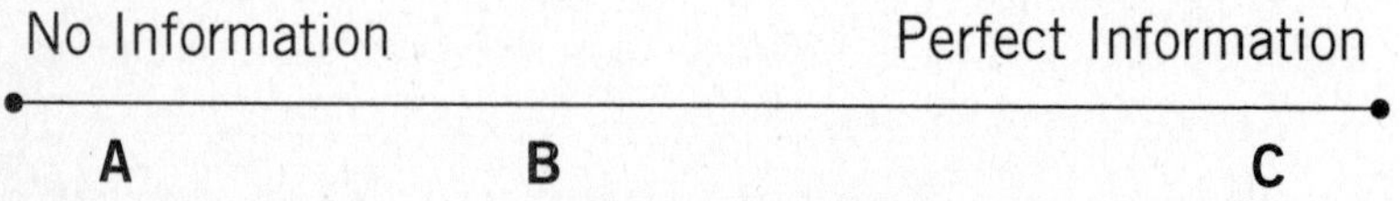

Point A is where the big bets are made. The people who make decisions at Point A are working with dreams, not data. Businesses built with Point A decisions are all-or-nothing propositions, and they end up on either magazine covers or bankruptcy dockets (sometimes both, but rarely in between).

Point C is where any idiot can make the right decision. It is very safe but does nothing to advance your business. Your competitors have already made the right call, and you are left shouting, "Me too!" to an empty room.

Point B is where you have some information but not nearly enough to be certain of the right call. This is where you want to make decisions. With time and experience, you want to move Point B as far to the left as you can while continuing to make more good decisions than bad ones.

Firefighters are Point B decision makers. If they waited for perfect information before they went into a burning building, they would never get hurt because they would never go in—there is no perfect information on a burning building. They would never save any lives either. If they went in with no information (no floor plans, no idea of who was inside or where), they would risk huge losses and would often be completely ineffective. Instead, they quickly gather all the information they can—on the building, the people, the situation—and make the best decisions they can. And they keep making decisions quickly as more information becomes available. With training and experience they push Point B to the left while continuing to win much more often than they lose.

Types of Decisions

Not all decisions are equal. It is important to recognize the different types of decisions you will encounter.

- **Foundational decisions.** Some decisions that are very difficult and expensive to change have significant long-term impact: choosing a business partner, for example. These decisions are poor candidates for making big bets; they are worth the time it takes to get better data. You should look for ways to keep these decisions as flexible and revocable as possible.

- **Trivial decisions.** These are the little decisions about the things that do not matter and do not have a significant impact: office supplies, party planning, cleaning service, etc. These decisions can be quite dangerous not because they matter but because they suck up your time. Delegate. Get other people to make these decisions.

  Trivial is a relative category. What is important is to understand what is trivial for you and hand that off to someone else for whom it may be nontrivial. Whether people you are handing things off to make more good or bad decisions on these things informs your nontrivial decisions about them.

- **Fatal decisions.** You need to stay alert for potentially fatal decisions so that they can be taken off the fast track and given more careful consideration. They cannot always be seen in advance, but as you increase the speed of your decision making, they are more frequently encountered. Breaking the law, shipping a product with a life-threatening defect, or bungling a high-profile opportunity are all things that can destroy a business.

  Businesses have an advantage over people in that a business

actually has a chance to recover from a fatal mistake, but only if they make corrective decisions instantly. Businesses have broken the law, caused deaths, and suffered humiliating blows to their reputation and still survived where an individual might have faced prison, loss of license or certification, or become unemployable.

It is best to anticipate and address potentially fatal decisions before you make them, but that is not always possible. When you do make a potentially fatal decision, it is usually because it appeared to be a different kind of decision. Once it has revealed itself, though, as something that could or should kill your business, you need to address it quickly in order to survive.

- **Every other decision.** The majority of decisions are grist for your mill. Grind them quickly and with as much wisdom as you can muster.

Learn to Be Content with Winning

When you have won, you have won. Enjoy it and move on to the next round. You do not need a 100% win any more than you need to be 100% correct in your decision making.

I'm not opposed to the business equivalent of pitching a perfect game. It's nice to bowl three hundred or to win all the points. But a perfect score isn't required in order to mark the win column, make a profit, and prepare to do it again.

When you accept that 51% is enough to win, you are freed from the dangerous compulsions of pursuing perfect victory. At best these compulsions waste your time and energy and keep you from pursuing the next win. At worst they lead to paranoia and ruin.

Richard Nixon won the 1972 presidential election by a landslide. He and his party didn't need the break-in or dirty tricks that led to the Watergate scandal in order to win. It was paranoia and a desire for a massive win that drove them. Fifty-one percent was enough to return Nixon to the White House, but it wasn't enough for them, so they pursued a bigger win, all the way to a massive loss.

These same destructive tendencies emerge in businesses all the time. Learn to be content. That means there are certain things you should never do.

Don't treat customers like criminals. Despite having a largely honest and law-abiding customer base, some businesses still treat all their customers like criminals. They implement policies, procedures, and technologies that presume customers are trying to steal their product or service. The measures they take rarely stop the real criminals but always annoy the honest majority. These customers are always on the lookout for an alternative.

Don't insist that others lose in order to feel like you have won. Not content to win part of a deal or to share a victory, some companies feel like they have not won until all their competitors have lost. While beating your competitors is great, creating "this deal isn't big enough for the two of us" scenarios can backfire. Next time, maybe you'll be the one who won't be allowed to share even a small piece of the deal.

Don't stomp ants. Like the physical world, the business world is full of parasites and ugly little insects. For every substantial business, there is a person or company that is abusing your policies, bad-mouthing you on the Internet, selling your products on the gray market, or otherwise annoying you to no end. Instead of just sending the occasional threatening attorney's letter, some companies become obsessed with stomping all the ants to death. It usually makes the stomping company look bad and accomplishes nothing in the end. New ants always show up.

Nobody likes a sore loser. What is worse is a sore winner.

A Dumpster diver once found a stack of overrun CD-ROMs behind our manufacturer's facility. He started selling these beta copies of our software product for a fraction of their retail price on the Internet. He refused to stop when we contacted him.

The suggested plan of action around our office ranged from a lawsuit to refusing to support customers who purchased these CDs to seeking compensation from the manufacturer. Anger was consuming us, and our plotting threatened to take even more time and resources. When we stopped and thought about how few disks he had to sell and that they represented less than 0.1% of our business, we realized that the winning move was to ignore him. We even offered to deduct what customers had paid him when they ordered our legitimate and updated version, turning his stolen-goods sale into hundreds of happy new customers for us.

100% Is a Goal, Not a Requirement

I would like to always make the right decision. I would like to never waste resources or make a bad investment. I would like to win every comparative review and address every item on my customers' wish lists.

I have learned that while those things are admirable goals, they can also be deadly traps. When I tried to avoid making any bad decisions, I was unable to make very many decisions at all. I cut myself off from serendipitous discoveries and slowed the pace of progress in my business.

When I tried to win every competitive matchup in every category, I found that I was investing large resources in checking off boxes on a chart that might be of interest to only a few customers. I used to think that every customer request was a feature requirement instead of just useful input for future releases.

Good may be the enemy of great,[1] but perfect is the enemy of progress. You will get further if you are willing to risk more along the way and to make decisions with imperfect information. Accept that you will take some losses and don't fret the little ones. Leave room in your world for others to win too.

Score the best win you can, but remember that 51% is all it takes.

21 Some People Are Your Greatest Assets

Most employees are interchangeable parts in your corporate machine.

Your employees may be great people. They may be smart, talented, and attractive. They may be volunteer firefighters, soccer coaches, and great parents. They may never be sick, never be late, and never fail to deliver on time. It doesn't matter. They are still a dime a dozen.

There are thousands, if not millions, of people who can do a good job in almost every position in your organization. It doesn't matter how specialized or how technical the position is. Lots of people can do it well enough. There is no shortage of good employees.

There is a terrible shortage of exceptional employees.

Good Is the Baseline

Before you invest in identifying, grooming, and retaining exceptional employees, you should make sure that you have already set "good" as your baseline standard for all employees. It is easy to get lazy or complacent or to develop a misguided sense of compassion that causes you to keep poor performers on staff. There is a right position somewhere for everyone. If you hire or retain people for a position that is wrong for them, you are doing them—and your own business—a terrible disservice.

It is a big world. Everyone can find something they do well, and you can find someone to do every job well. There is no excuse for having less than a good employee in every position.

Why Do You Need Exceptional Employees?

You need as many exceptional employees as you can get because good isn't good enough to get ahead. In a world full of people who can do a good job in the right position, you need some people who are better than good in order to beat the competition and move up to the next level.

Your competitors are putting out a quality product, just like you. Your competitors have pleasant, helpful salespeople, just like you. Your competitors are fully staffed with good people, just like you.

You need an advantage. You need something exceptional.

Exceptional Is the Extra

Exceptional employees aren't better people or people in specific jobs. They are people with something *extra.* Many people with something extra have it hidden away, or else they are putting it to use in some other area of their life. Exceptional employees are the intersection of the right person and the right job in such a way that the heretofore untapped *extra*—extra spirit, potential, effort, or genius—is released in their work.

Exceptional employees are exceptional in lots of different ways. There isn't a single quality that makes someone an exceptional employee, and very often, an employee who is exceptional in one way is below average in another—that can be the price of excellence.

Some of the ways in which employees can be exceptional include the following.

- **Attitude.** Call it charisma. Call it personality. Call it that little spark. Some people have the whatever-it-is that everyone likes. There is enormous business value in likability; it sells products, improves morale, and even backs off creditors.

- **Talent.** In every discipline there are the competent and the talented. The competent engineer or programmer or technician works the process and gets good results. The talented one gets better results faster and develops the new processes for the competent to use in the future.
- **Creativity.** There are lots of designers who can do nice, attractive work. There are some designers who can create products or packaging that command attention and compel purchases. In every creative field—words, music, art, food, etc.—there are people whose work floats in the clouds far above the merely good.
- **Initiative.** There are people who do what they are supposed to do. And then there are people who do what needs to be done. You can't have enough of these people: the employee who picks up the trash on the sidewalk on his way in the front door; the employee who helps the customer who shows up just after closing time; the employee who learns the new technology or process before you know you will be using it.
- **Genius.** Some people see things no one else can see. They make huge intellectual leaps into the future where they discover new products, new markets, and new ideas.
- **Versatility.** There are people who can do a good job in any position: the salesperson who can help out in the warehouse; the technician who can staff the booth at the trade show.

The most exceptional employees are investing themselves in the business. It is not that they have no life outside of work or even that they are working extra hours. It is that they are bringing to work everything they have to offer instead of simply what is necessary to do the job.

One of my noncommissioned salespeople spent an exhausting

couple of days at a conference on the other side of the country. On the last night of the conference, he heard about a possible sales opportunity with an organization more than a hundred miles away from the conference. The next morning, on his own initiative, he made an appointment and drove two hours to a meeting and two hours back before catching his afternoon flight home. Then he demonstrated our product to the people sitting next to him on the plane, and he took a credit card order at 30,000 feet.

> Exceptional employees work and care for the business as if they owned it.

That is an exceptional employee. That is the kind of employee you wish you could clone.

How to Identify the Cloning Candidates

Many exceptional employees know that they are exceptional, and they make sure you know it too. You won't have any problem identifying these shameless self-promoters, and there is nothing wrong with that.

Other exceptional employees are working quietly in your organization and may be off your radar. They can remain hidden because they don't report directly to you or even because you see them as just one part of a larger team of good employees.

One way to smoke out the exceptional people is to create a list of all your employees in the order in which you would eat them if your entire company was stranded for weeks on a remote, snowy mountaintop after your chartered plane crashed on the way home from a powerful weekend of bonding and team-building rope-course exercises.* Or, more likely and only slightly less cold, the order in which you would lay them off if compelled by a downturn in your business.

*This is, of course, facetious. The scenario would never happen. And besides, if it did, your employees would certainly eat you first.

Have department managers build the same list for their departments. The resulting list is a handy tool at the bottom of which you will find yourself and your most exceptional employees. The list is also a very dangerous document to leave sitting on the printer. Even if you are good about picking up your printouts, it is probably better not to title the list "Employee Roster by Expendability."

Another good way to identify exceptional employees is to ask their coworkers. In addition to soliciting feedback one-on-one, every year I conduct an anonymous survey of my employees. One of the questions on the survey asks them to identify coworkers whom they think are underappreciated. This has helped bring to my attention exceptional employees who were working in important but low-profile positions.

How to Treat Your Exceptional Employees

The best way to take care of and keep your exceptional employees is to be an exceptional employer. The best employees want to work for a business where they are treated with respect and dignity and where there is a great work environment.

Your exceptional employees should be getting something extra, though. Sometimes that something extra is money: a higher salary or a bigger bonus. More often it is flexibility and freedom: an extra benefit that is both recognition of their extraordinary value and room to exercise their special qualities.

Inside my company, we have found lots of ways to reward exceptional employees besides money though we have spread around no small amount of cash as well.

- **The coolest tools.** Everybody gets the equipment they need to do their job. Some people get more equipment than they need to do their job. Like the wide-screen laptop with the DVD player instead of the perfectly adequate simpler one.

- **Choice of projects.** Whenever possible exceptional employees get to choose from available projects before they are assigned. Not only are they happier with what they are working on, they usually choose the projects where they can do the best work.
- **Flexible schedule.** If the position allows it, exceptional employees are given control over their own schedules. They work the hours they want and are trusted to manage their own flextime.
- **Recognition.** Tell exceptional employees that they are exceptional. Recognize them personally, one-on-one, and praise them to their coworkers, your customers, and to their families.* Being in the spotlight onstage is uncomfortable for some people, so know when to hire a band and when to acknowledge quietly.
- **Freedom to play.** Talented and creative employees want time to explore and invent. Days allocated to vaguely defined projects or "research" give them room to grow; employees see it as a reward, and the business reaps benefits from their growth.

Don't play favorites with your children. Do play favorites with your employees.

What About Exceptional Employees Who Are Jerks?

A recurring question to the business magazine advice columnists goes something like this: "I have this super salesperson who is my consistent number one performer. The problem is that while he is always nice to clients, he is rude to everyone else in the office. I have

*Company picnics and holiday parties are where you meet the families. Don't pass up the chance to acknowledge and praise your exceptional employees in front of the people who matter most to them.

tried talking to him to no effect. He is killing the company morale, but I can't afford to fire him because he sells twice as much as the next salesperson."

Fire the jerks.

Don't move them to another department. Don't isolate them from their coworkers. Get rid of them. You spend too many hours of your life in your business to be wasting your time with jerks. Don't waste your good employees' time that way either, or you will lose them and be stuck with a business full of jerks.

Time and Place

As your business grows, you will find that your idea of what (and who) makes for an exceptional employee changes. The versatile, freewheeling do-it-all who was essential during your start-up phase may not adapt to the necessary more formal processes of a larger organization. The simply average telephone salesperson might emerge as an amazing field representative when given a chance to get out of the office.

You can't build a business with only exceptional employees. For one thing, there aren't enough of them. To build a business that can scale up and survive the coming and going of employees over the years, you will need to develop processes and systems that reflect your way of doing things. These systems need to be developed so that good employees—the important and renewable resources from which you build an organization—can learn them quickly and execute them well.

Some of the exceptional employees you will have the privilege of working with will be exceptional in their ability to work within your systems. Many will be exceptional in ways that cause them to chafe under the constraints of your systems. Their creative energy, thirst for knowledge, or ability to see better solutions can make them seem more like troublemakers than exceptional employees.

Pay attention. Keep an eye out for the exceptional employees who are in danger of being pushed aside by changes in the organization and for the potentially exceptional employees who could be revealed by a change in assignment.

- **If you are formalizing your systems as part of your growth, watch out for the exceptional employees who might be seeing reduced opportunities for exercising their special talents in the new, tighter framework.** You may want to give these employees new job descriptions and projects in new areas where they can have the freedom to innovate. You may want to put them in charge of developing and refining the systems so that they see them as places to contribute rather than as limitations on their creativity.
- **Open up special projects and assignments to the whole organization.** Let your employees volunteer to try assignments in a variety of new areas without having to give up their current position. If you don't provide the opportunity, you may never know that the good employee with Job A could have been exceptional with Job B. They may not know it themselves.
- **Develop a farm team inside your organization.** In my company, the customer service department sees the most new employees. That is partially because it is a large department with an entry-level wage. It is also because the other departments are always poaching its staff. The hard work of telephone customer service weeds out the lazy, the rude, and the uninterested. It quickly reveals good employees, exceptional employees, and those who might be exceptional in another position.

Good Isn't Good Enough Anymore

We live in a world of abundant, affordable quality. The days of getting ahead by doing a good job, building a good product, or providing a good service are over. Your business needs to be exceptional in some way, or it is doomed to drift forever on the sea of homogeneity.

Today it is almost impossible to maintain an advantage in process, materials, or design for very long. The only long-term advantages are the exceptional employees who find, invent, and apply those things. These exceptional employees are your greatest assets.

22 Business Is a Serious Game

I entered the world of business with all the enthusiasm of a little kid.

Actually, I entered it as a little kid.

My grandfather and father were both entrepreneurs, so running a business always seemed like something that I could do too. Even more important, I was impatient, and businessman seemed like a career I could embark on while still in elementary school.

Starting at six years old, I was selling things to friends at school and setting up sales stands in front of the house. At ten, with my mother's help, I set up beehives behind our suburban home so that I could go into the honey business.

Bob's Honey was my first real business. While waiting for my hive to build up production, I sourced honey from two states. I managed inventory, produced marketing materials, and tracked sales using the earliest computer spreadsheets. I was "playing business," but with real money and real toys.

When wild bears knocked out my supply line, I was crushed. Wild raspberry honey from the backwoods of Maine was my premium-priced bestseller. Without it, I was just another commodity clover honey supplier. Bob's Honey closed down.

But I had been bit by the business bug. (Or, rather, stung by the business bee.) By the time I started a software company at age fourteen, I was fully caught up in learning the business game. I subscribed to *Fortune* and the *Wall Street Journal*. I read every business biography and history I could find. I hung out in the offices of my father's company and rode along on sales trips whenever I could. I focused on the excitement of business success, not the details of business operations.

Business was a lark. It was easy and fun and, since student-living-at-home was my day job, it was risk free. It was still just an adventure when, at twenty, I quit a great job at Microsoft to cofound Logos Research Systems, Inc.

Immediate success and rapid growth fueled my enthusiasm for the entrepreneurial life and puffed up my ego. Ever-increasing sales hid many mistakes and deferred tough decisions. There was lots of pressure, but it was all part of the game. I was still "playing business."

I remember the first time I felt the responsibility of my job. I was starting to see the early signs of trouble in the business. I stood up on a picnic table to say a few words at the company picnic and looked out at more than one hundred people—employees and their family members. Our business had been a great game to me, but it was a livelihood to these employees, and it supported their families. It was not a game to them.

Within a year, I was laying off some of those employees. Our growth had slowed, and my mistakes had caught up with me. The business sank lower and lower and with it my confidence and my enthusiasm for the great game of business.

The lowest point was when, just after another painful round of layoffs, I went to a local business group meeting that the organizer had insisted I attend. It turned out that our new and difficult circumstances were not well known: I was handed a plaque proclaiming our company "Business of the Year."

I hid the plaque in shame and never told anyone at the office.

Lessons from the Game

By God's grace, and with the help of some incredible people, we slowly turned the business around. Our financial circumstances forced me to learn discipline and focus and humility.* I learned to emphasize profitability, to pay attention to operations, and to be wiser in hiring and firing.

I saw that my childish approach to business as simply an adventure game was the result of too much focus on stories of heroic business success and not enough attention to how the heroes kept their businesses alive and growing day-to-day. The businesses I admired were not successful because they were led by heroes; those entrepreneurs were heroes because they led their businesses to success.

This book is about the lessons I have learned the hard way while growing up in business. It is about the rules I have extracted from those lessons. If this book has a tinge of paranoia to it, if I am telling you what *not to do* as much as what *to do*, it is because I have been to the edge, and it scared me. I now see survival as a prerequisite to success. You do not get a chance to scale the summit if you freeze to death in base camp the night before.

Seek Professional Help

The book of Proverbs says that there is safety in a multitude of counselors.[1] *That* is good advice. Some of the ways in which I have sought a multitude of counselors are outlined in this book: visiting in person, reading widely, and buying lunch. You should do the same.

My advice contains some universal business truths. Cash really is king. But for every rule I espouse, there is a successful business somewhere doing just the opposite and counting it as a virtue. And for them, it may be. There may be a different set of rules for you too.

Don't just take my advice. I could be wrong. Instead, look at your own experiences, take what you already know and weigh that against my advice and the advice of others.

One of the best investments I have made in business, and in

---

*I have more to learn of all three. Ask my wife.

getting wise counsel, has been joining groups of other entrepreneurs. The first was a local CEO roundtable that held informal monthly meetings, and the second was the local chapter of the international Young Entrepreneurs Organization ("YEO").

The other businesspeople in these groups gave me encouragement and advice. Most importantly, we shared our experiences of success and failure. From these shared experiences, we all got ideas, inspiration, and warnings.

Find a group of business peers with whom you can share and learn. I cannot recommend YEO strongly enough; if YEO is not the right fit for you, then find the group that is. This is one of the best investments you can make in your business.

The lessons you need to learn in order to make your business a success are all around you. Some are in this book, some will be in a story you hear from another businessperson, and some you will have to learn the hard way on your own.

Drop Me a Line

I wish you the best in your business education and invite you to participate in my own; it never ends. I would like to hear about your business experiences and the lessons you have learned. I would like to hear which of the lessons in this book have been helpful to you and which have been counter to your experience.

You can reach me at bob@firesomeonetoday.com and online at www.firesomeonetoday.com.

Acknowledgments

This book started as nothing more than a title—the three-word lesson I learned first and best from the shared experiences of my friends in Forum 3 of the Seattle Chapter of the Young Entrepreneurs Organization.

As the list of lessons grew, it was my wife, Audra, who encouraged me to put them into a book. Our friends Michael and Hayley DiMarco helped me shape a proposal, and my YEO forum helped me commit to the project. My children, Jacob and Kathleen, gave me permission to steal away from their evenings and weekends the time to write it.

Eli Evans, Rick Brannan, and Vincent Setterholm went above and beyond as my sounding board and first-pass editors, showing up weekly with detailed notes and sparing no just criticism—and no unjust barb. Our dinners were the best part of the process.

Brian Hampton championed the book at Nelson Business and helped refine the presentation; Paula Major was wonderfully thorough and patient in polishing the text. Everyone at Thomas Nelson Publishers has been great to work with.

Without the friendship and partnership of Kiernon Reiniger, I would never have embarked on this business adventure. Without the hard work and incredible support of our team at Logos Research Systems, Inc.—past and present—the adventure would have been more dramatic and a whole lot shorter. Logos employees, I am sorry for all the wrong turns on the road!

Thanks to everyone who contributed the stories and connections and insights and comments behind this book: Dave Adamson, Ed Ball, Adam Brotman, Rud Browne, Fred Crosetto, Mark Dealy, Jeff Dennis, Bob Diforio, Peter Economy, Anne-Marie Faiola, Robert Friske, Paul Grey, Ken Hey, Wayne Kinde, Rand Lien, Brock Mansfield, Bob Margulis, Dan Pritchett, Pamela Rhodes, Richard Rhodes, Andy Sack, Susan Schreter, Brian Scudamore, Andy Skipton, Jerry Skipton, Phil Stoner, Bob Thordarson, and Tony White. To those I have missed, please forgive me.

Most of all, I want to thank my parents, Dale and Jenni Pritchett, who encouraged me in business all my life and who taught me the really important lessons of life. My father was the third partner in our business, and he gave me a rare and fantastic gift: the freedom to lead. He allowed me to choose the path; to fail, learn, and grow. In our years of working together, his superior wisdom as a father and businessman was always available but never asserted. No son could be more blessed in working with his father.

Endnotes

Chapter 3 Nobody Loves Your Baby Like You Do

1. Col. Harland A. Sanders, *Life as I Have Known It Has Been Finger Lickin' Good* (Carol Stream, IL: Creation House, 1974), 115–16.
2. http://folklore.org/StoryView.py?project=Macintosh&story=Reality_Distortion_Field.txt.

Chapter 10 Profit Is Why You Are in Business

1. Robert Hayes, quoted in "Riding the Range in Wireless Country," TheStreet.com, December 12, 2000, http://www.thestreet.com/pf/comment/tish/1208866.html and Carly Fiorina, quoted in "*HP* Is More Than Just Hardware," IDG News Service, November 4, 2004, http://www.itworld.com/Man/3828/041104hphardware/.

Chapter 17 Press Is Yours If You Ask—and If You Want It

1. "The Merchant of Bay Ridge," *Forbes*, December 27, 2004, http://www.forbes.com/free_forbes/2004/1227/080.html.

Chapter 18 In Acquisitions, the Buyer Is the Loser

1. Alibris, Inc., March 3, 2004, Form S-1. SEC/EDGAR, http://www.sec.gov/edgar.shtml.
2. *Fortune*, February 5, 2001, http://www.fortune.com/fortune/subs/article/0,15114,370682,00.html. "'HR buys are becoming more prominent. If a

company can buy another firm cheap enough and pick up 50 or 100 networking engineers who have skills in key technologies, it's not a bad idea,' says Mark Shafir, codirector of investment banking at Thomas Weisel Partners. These deals, though, will work only if the talent can be retained, he adds."

Chapter 20 Winning Takes 51%

1. "Good is the enemy of great" is the opening statement of Jim Collins's best-selling book *Good to Great* (New York: Harper Collins, 2004).

Chapter 22 Business Is a Serious Game

1. Proverbs 11:14; 15:22; 20:18; 24:6.

About the Author

A third-generation entrepreneur, Bob Pritchett started his first business at age six. In high school, he ran a software company that sold to the Fortune 500. He left high school early to attend university, and at age nineteen, he left university to join Microsoft as one of its youngest program managers.

At age twenty, Pritchett left Microsoft to cofound Logos Research Systems, Inc. Over the years, he has led his company through high growth, a nearly fatal IPO attempt, and back to solid, debt-free profitability. He has been invited to speak to industry and academic groups around the world and has been featured in publications ranging from the *Whidbey News Times* to *BusinessWeek*. He is also a 2005 winner of the Ernst & Young Entrepreneur of the Year Award.

Bob Pritchett is married with two children and is the president/CEO of Logos Research Systems, Inc., and managing director of its South African subsidiary.

For additional resources and information about Bob and his book, *Fire Someone Today,* please visit **www.firesomeonetoday.com.**